Before Common Ground

Living the American Dream:
The Journey of an Immigrant American Football Player

by Patrick A. Morrison, MSW

DORRANCE
PUBLISHING CO
EST. 1920
PITTSBURGH, PENNSYLVANIA 15238

Dorrance Publishing Co
585 Alpha Drive
Pittsburgh, PA 15238
Visit our website at www.dorrancebookstore.com

ISBN: 978-1-4809-8938-2
eISBN: 978-1-4809-8912-2

Loving Acknowledgements

To My Wife Desiree who has stood with me at my lowest and highest points, thank you.

To my children: London, Langston and Malkelm Morrison. Dad has done his best in spite of his own experiences to grant you the opportunity to obtain your dreams.

To all my coaches who has guided and counseled me on my life's journey thank you.

Lastly, to my Mother, Imogene Lucilda Morrison-Bailey, thank you for crossing the Atlantic seas in search of a better future for yourself and me. Without you, this book would not be possible.

Chapter One

In the Beginning

As I reflect, the light shining bright above my head was the first memory I have of life, as I know it. I must have been laying in a crib or bed as a baby, because I don't recall being able to move away from the light to shield it from my eyes or call out to have someone turn it off. I do remember the room; besides the single bulb hanging from the ceiling, I remember the room being sparsely furnished and the walls being a dark hue. As I reflect fifty years later, the room was of humble and minimal furnishings. This was the place where my life journey would begin, far beyond any dream or future hopes my little mind was experiencing at that time. I am sure the reader will understand my memories of fifty years ago will have some missing moments and possibly some questionable dates. I believe the reader understands that after fifty years, one cannot expect to remember every moment and situation accurately. Additionally, my memory has been compromised over time, which could be caused by time itself or from the many collisions I encountered later on this football journey.

My first memory of human interaction was with a woman who I later realized was my mother. I recall her face as always smiling brightly with a sense of love about her, like an angel, as she stood in the kitchen cooking up the morning breakfast and preparing the evening meal. I remember the constant morning breakfast would be porridge, otherwise known as "corn meal porridge." It was made with corn meal flour and water and stirred until the water absorbed into the corn meal. Another traditional West Indian breakfast meal was liver with salt fish fritters and ripe plantains. I can smell them now as I reminisce on that time long ago. I never recalled my mother heading off to work while I was a child; all I ever knew was that I was in a room; I was alive; and Mom was there. I vividly remember two significant moments in my life as a child remaining with me to this day. Today it's a running joke within my immediate family and an example of how simple minded I was, but I was resourceful as a child in that I associated water with fire quickly. This is an age of electronics where high-tech gadget games exist for today's youth to amuse them and occupy their time, but there was a time when children played outside for much of the time, playing games such as soccer, cricket, baseball, and throwing and kicking the football around. It was also a time on those lazy, early morning Saturdays where boys would stay inside and play with their racing tracks or green army men. The latter is where my story begins.

I must have been five or six years old, because by this time my environment (living arrangements) was bright, comfortable, and roomy. I remember my mother being in the kitchen, as usual, doing her "mother thing," cooking up the evening dinner—which probably was the usual meal of "cook food": ripe banana, yams, carrots, rice and peas, and ox tails. As she cooked, I was in the front room of our upstairs flat playing with my race track. I remember the flat being upstairs because at some point in my childhood years I fell down the steps, which lead to the door leading out to the hallway, to the steps of the family living room beneath us. I remember crying and my mother coming down to rescue me after my ill-fated fall.

On this particular sunny yet cool, lazy Saturday morning I decided to play with my track. I had to decide what figuration I wanted my cars to drive around that day. My choices: the usual figure eight, oval, or curvy oval. I chose the figure eight. The figure eight was the most exciting because that meant your track and car had to go around obstacles and maintain speed without it going off the track. What obstacles would I choose? Like I mentioned, the day was bright and sunny but cold outside, and my mother had the kerosene heater going in the room to keep the room warm for me to play as she worked in the kitchen.

"That's it," I said in my childish mind.

The figure eight would look good going around the heater, weaving its way around danger and coming through unscathed. So, I set up the track without touching the heater because I knew it was hot. The room was small: just big enough for a single reclining chair, a table with a black and white TV on top, and maybe a love-seat sofa. I believe there was also a little table next to the door that supported fancy glasses for those "special occasions."

So here I go playing with my racetrack, watching the cars go around and around the track, momentarily losing sight of each car as they passed behind the heater. I was enjoying myself, but after awhile, watching the cars go around and around and putting the cars back on the track time after time as they kept falling off the track became a little boring for this six-year old. I guess my driving skills weren't as together as I'd thought.

At this age, children don't really have an acute sense of velocity and how to control speed, and I sure didn't, but it was fun. After watching the cars going around the same pattern awhile, I realized that I wanted to change the configuration to something different. I decided to change the design to a curvy oval. To do this, I needed more space to expand the size of the track, which would require me to move the heater out of the way and place it in another location—preferably in the middle of this new exciting design. As I picked up the heater by its fragile handle, I realized (too late) that the heater, which had a clasp holding the top of it together and that protected the lightened wicks from sparking onto the floor, was not clasped at all. This new revelation quickly resulted in Kerosene dripping onto the floor, next to the recliner chair that had a cotton cushion seat. Immediately the chair caught on fire and the room began to fill with smoke! As my family continually reminds me today and as I, too, reflect on that moment, I had remained cool and calm. I not sure if I really knew the significance of what was happening at the time, but my actions going forward would lead you to believe that I did not. As the flames spread across the cushion, I made my way out of the room and headed towards the kitchen where my mother was still working on our meal for the day. She was unaware of what was happening in her front room. As I entered the kitchen, I remember looking into my mother's eyes and asking for a glass of water, "Can I have water, please?"

It definitely is a mother's sixth sense that enables them to know things that others don't. "What do you need water for?" she asked.

I replied, "to drink something."

Something about that response did not sit well with her, as she immediately looked behind me up the three steps that led to the short hallway and to the living area of the flat. She noticed the flames and smoke and ran towards the smoke as I ran behind her and watched her attempt to put the flames out with a bed sheet. She thought quickly, as she opened the window and threw the flamed filled cotton cushion out of the window and smothered the flames that had made their way onto the carpet. At this moment, I was still in shock and didn't know what to do. Up to that point in my young life, I don't remember ever having been disciplined by my mother for anything I had done wrong. I want to believe that I was a good child, but that day I witnessed my first discipline. You would think after nearly burning down the house, my mother would spank me or even implore corporal punishment. I tried to explain to her the configuration I was trying to make and how it was supposed to be better, but she was not having or hearing any of it.

She scolded me in a rough Jamaican accent, letting me know, "don't du dat."

I remember feeling bad about what had happened and that I ended up sitting on a bed in a room by myself with the door closed.

There was another woman in my life during this time: my older sister, Pauline. She was born in Jamaica, WI, to my mother's first mate (who is not my father). Even though we are separated by eleven years and had different fathers, she was always there for me when I needed a big sister to comfort and protect me when mom wasn't around. This fire incident is the first example of the love my sister has for me, and from that time on I realized I could always call on her and she would not pass judgment but would just provide support and guidance. Because she was so much older than me, we really didn't hang out with each other, nor were our ages close enough for me to be her little brother who her girlfriends thought was "cute" enough to want to get to know. Pauline worked at a shoe store as a teenager and during the fire episode she was at work. By time she got home that evening, the fire trucks had come and gone, and I was still in my bedroom, sitting on the bed, alone. She must have asked mom what happened before she entered the room, because she entered cautiously, anticipating to still find me on the bed.

She came in and sat next to me and told me, "It's okay, but next time ask for help and if you need something, don't be scared to ask."

These kind simple words meant so much to me after being alone and not hearing a comforting voice from a loved one. She made sure I understood the seriousness of the situation, which I did, and she promised me she would bring home a new pair of shoes for me. That put a big smile on my face after so many hours of despair. But now I was about to get a new pair of shoes from my big sister, and I was as happy as a lark in anticipation. Two or so weeks later, my sister came home and opened a new box of hush puppy brown shoes. The shoes were a big deal because we didn't have much. Mom was a single parent trying to raise a young boy and a teenage girl on a single minimal salary. Later in life, I would do whatever I could to relieve the financial pressure off her, the same way my sister did.

I mentioned there are two specific memories as a young child that I recall that were significant. The first was the racing track fire and the second was when I was indirectly introduced to England's most cherished and honored musical groups. Somewhere between falling down the steps and burning down the house, I also played with my Beatles guitar. I recall it being beige in color with multi-color strings, and the face of it had the images of Paul, Ringo, John, and George. Before I knew anything about music, I knew the Beatles, and I would play my little Beatles guitar all the time as I sat in the front room by myself. Later in life, and as I became involved in church activities, the guitar became my instrument of choice. There isn't much more I remember about that guitar, other than the images of England's super group. Now as an adult I recognize their impact on the music industry and social significance. As for memories that shaped my thoughts, perceptions, and later my perspective on race and how I reflect on my life journey, I can honestly say I've been exposed to enough to make a good assessment about a few things that are relevant. At this point in my life, and I am assuming that I was still in my formidable years, around six or seven years old, living free-willed with no worries in the world—just playing and enjoying life. It is also the time when I had my first encounter with *hate*.

The flat where my mother, sister and I lived was off a main road that ran alongside a narrow side street. If the reader knows London at all, you know the streets are narrow, and the homes favor the row homes you might find in Baltimore, MD, Washington D.C, or Philadelphia, PA. Our home was along this narrow street and along the street stood a long, red stone wall. The red stone wall ran mostly throughout the entire street, dividing the street from the backyards of the flats on the other street. At the top of the wall, cement is held in place and edges of broken glass protrude from the top of the wall. I guess this was a security deterrent for intruders to not jump over the wall. For entertainment I would kick my football against this wall, as I would try to sharpen my kicking skills to be like Pele or England's own, Johnny Best. Before there was Messi and Renaldo, these were the two best footballers you would ever want to see that represented Brazil and England. One day I was kicking my ball against the red brick wall and I accidently kicked it over and into the backyard of a home whose backyard ran along the narrow street. I wasn't sure how I would get it, but I stood around to see if I would see the owner and have him or her throw it back over the glass-tipped wall. I stood there for a while when, finally, the lady of the house came out. I yelled as loud as I could until I got her attention. The lady turned around and looked at me over her red wall. She was a Caucasian lady with rosy cheeks. She had a pleasant smile on her face as she came closer to the wall's edge. I explained, to the best of my ability, that my ball went over the wall, and inquired as to whether she had seen it. She turned around, bent down, and disappeared out of sight. I initially thought that she was getting back to her business and didn't want to be bothered with this little kid kicking balls into her garden. However, seconds later my ball reappeared flying over the wall and heading my way. I never saw her throw the ball over for me to say *thank you*: I just saw the ball. After picking the ball up, I noticed the ball had been deflated. Not sure what happened but I was out of luck. I went up stairs and showed my mother, and she told me that I should be careful and not kick the ball "over those peoples' walls; we don't know them, and they will pop it on purpose." I didn't know what to think of that statement because up to that point I had never experienced hate or racism. When my sister returned home from the shoe store that day, I told her what happened. Without hesitation she gave me a few shillings to buy another ball at the corner store! That store sold everything, from candy, socks, mops, to even footballs. So, I ran across the street (from what I can remember) and purchased another one. I took it out of the plastic bag and went straight to the red wall with the glass edges. I began kicking the ball against the wall again. I kicked as hard as I could, for a child of five or six years old. I kicked the ball again and as I watched the power and height of this kick as it left my foot, I knew again I was in trouble as it sailed over the wall. My heart fell to my feet. I now felt I was going to get in trouble by my mother (for sure this time), my sister, and the old, rosy red-cheeked woman living behind the red wall. Nervously, I called out again for the lady over the red wall. This time I saw a big, burly, rosy red-cheeked Caucasian man in the backyard. He didn't look as welcoming as did the rosy red-cheeked woman whom I had encountered earlier. As I called out to get his attention, I told him that my ball went over his wall and asked if he could please throw it back. He looked at me, then looked away, then bent down and was out of view just as the rosy-cheeked woman was when she went out of view. My heart now was beating faster. I was scared and worried what my mom would say if I told her what had happened again. The man reappeared in less time than the lady before. He appeared with the ball in his hand, which appeared fully inflated. I was happy about that because it meant I didn't have to ask Big Sis for money again and that I could continue playing without anyone knowing what I did again.

My hopes dissipated. The burly man with the rosy red cheeks had a knife in his hand and spurted curse words, saying that I should keep my balls out of his yard; I watched him stab the ball and rip it open with his large knife (large from the perspective of the eyes of a five- or six- year-old child) and throw it back over the fence at me. I was shocked beyond belief that my ball was cut up by the rosy red-cheeked man and that I now had nothing to play with. In England, there is no baseball, basketball, or football. I wasn't yet introduced to Rugby or cricket. Besides, what was I going to say to my mother once I returned upstairs to the flat? She told me what not to do again and I did it. My sister told me to be careful and I wasn't. So, I decided to go in and face the judge: my mother. As I took that long trek up the steps leading to our apartment, I wondered how I would tell my mother what happened. As I opened the door, my smiling mother greeted me. She wanted to know if I was okay because she was just heading out to check on me. She must have forgotten what I was actually doing outside, because she never asked me about the whereabouts of my ball, and I never brought it up. I told her I was tired from running around and that I came in for some water. I asked her if she knew where my guitar was. She said it was in my room on my bed. I went in my room, sat on my bed with my Beatles guitar, and that was the last time I ever bought or played English football.

Growing up in England those few early years turned out to be quite impactful on my life, as I later came to realize. My friends and family were limited to three or four families that had migrated from Jamaica less than ten years earlier. The one friend I remember to this day was Johnny. I remember he was my playmate and his mom and mine were best friends. Ms. Sara was her name and her home was a place of enjoyment and conversation between the families. To this day, my mother maintains her communications with Ms. Sara and checks to see how the kids are doing. The other impactful childhood friend I had was my cousin Clive "Clyde" Vaughan. I remember growing up in the same house and playing and running. Clive was older than me by four years, but that didn't stop us from building a close brotherly bond. I'm not sure why we became so close, maybe because I didn't have a brother of my own to play "boy games" with, or maybe the time our families spent together made our relationship feel more like brothers than anything else. His sisters, Valery and Beverly are one year younger and one year older than me, respectively, but growing up, Val and I were the closest and played a lot together, as she had a very outgoing, take-the-initiative-and-take-control type of personality. In our teenage years, the relationship with Clive grew into a more special bond that set the stage for success in our family.

These early years in my life were good times. It was a time of growth from a toddler to a young boy, playing, establishing friends and family bonds, and becoming more self-aware that I am a human being living amongst other human beings and that I have feelings and emotions that can affect the outcome of how I approach or avoid my experiences later in life. I went from a dim lit room of unawareness and emptiness to a life of engagement, love, and exploration. Little did I know that within a short time of this existence and self-awareness my life would change, and the experiences I was experiencing would have a profound effect on my mental status, self-esteem and abilities.

Chapter Two

Dear Momma

Those early years at home were great. My life journey was still new, fresh, and uneventful—not at all that complicated. One thing that was constant from the very beginning was church. I didn't know if I was Baptist, Catholic, Protestant, or Methodist; all I knew was that I was there all the time. (I will return to this subject in a few more lines.) My mother and her family while growing up in Jamaica believed in the Almighty God, and a strong spiritual conviction of going to church daily was very important to that conviction and was part of one's spiritual faith and saving grace from the eternal hell fire. So, when my mom came to me one day and told me that I would be staying with my uncle, her brother, and his wife for a little while, I believed I would be staying with people that believed in God and that life would go on as normal and my spiritual growth would continue to grow positively under their care. Mom made the decision to follow other family members who migrated to the USA in the late sixties and early seventies with the hopes of finding opportunities and living the advertised "American Dream."

Around the summer of 1971, at the age of six, my mother left me to live with the "God-fearing," church-going, and filled-with-the-Holy-Spirit home of my Uncle Eddie and Aunt Louise. At six-years old, you're sad that your mom is leaving you, but not thinking it will be for a long time. At age six, a long time could be a couple of hours, so a couple of years felt like a life time. In addition, I was in the home of my uncle with himself, his wife, Louise, and their two sons, Cleave and Terrance, so my expectations were that it would be safe, and I would just have to wait until mom returned. The boys—my cousins—were older than me. Cleve was already a teenager in some sort of accounting institution, and Terrance was a working electrical mechanic. When I think back to then, I realize that the time they spent with me wasn't necessarily to educate and guide me into being a young man, but rather to protect me from events and persons that I would eventually experience in the house under the supervision of my Aunt Louise, which would change my life for a lifetime. My Aunt Louise was a church-going, Bible-verse-reciting, non-sparing-the-rod overseer. She was a stout, brown-skinned, firm, and stern affect of a woman. Like most black families in the seventies and eighties, we attended church at least five days a week and twice on Sunday. I always wondered how God could be so good, but his "saints" so angry. I was put in the Gleaner band for the little children, so we could learn our Bible verses and sing to "the glory of his name." Many of the spiritual rituals are nothing new for the "Black experience," however I soon learned that *not* meeting the expectations of an obedient child would bring the wrath of God upon me, and the outcome of this wrath would eventually be the burning force that was buried in my consciousness and soul, and eventually would lead and motivate me later in life.

We were Pentecostal—a denomination that strongly held close to the teachings of the Old Testament as the foundation of our faith. Women should not wear pants—no makeup, head coverings, etc. Discipline of the child is paramount because the child is the representative of the family and the church and if the child goes astray, it's reflective of the family and the church. I was initially a happy child that loved music and playing with other children and just living life. In church I would sit next to the band and listen to "God's music" being played by the guitar and drummer, mixed with the Caribbean vibes and sounds of the Jamaican members of the church. Prayer time was always exciting, because when the "Holy Ghost" would take over, the theatrics were something to see, especially from the eyes of a six-year old. Usually in the middle of this spiritual experience was Aunt Louise. She took her religion seriously. So seriously, I don't believe I ever saw her smile—well, never at me. Uncle Eddie was in church as well, ushering, singing, praying, and striving to be a righteous man. He was a good man—engaging, hard-working, and had a wonderful laugh. He was always there for me ensuring that I was safe and allowed me to experience the wonders of life that God created, as he knew and saw it. In addition to being a master carpenter, he was a photographer. He would bring me along on his photo shoots and allow me to go in his darkroom as he developed pictures. It was amazing to see the pictures come alive from a blank piece of glossy white paper. He spent time with me when he could get away from working and building things. He was a master carpenter and his skills were something for one's eyes to behold. He did what he could, when he could, to teach me and show me things that would help me grow into a happy little boy.

Things changed however as the household became *normal* with me, their new housemate. My sister didn't want to come live with my aunt and uncle because she didn't like Aunt Louise. I found out later from Pauline that she knew Aunt Louise was mean and not a nice person, so Mom placed my sister with a best friend, Mrs. Sara. I saw my sister one other time after her placement with Mrs. Sara and wouldn't see her for the next thirty years. I recall my first physical discipline from Aunt Louise was in church where I got my first "pinch." I think many children growing up in the black church can relate to this. The black church can begin with nine o'clock Sunday school and end at two or three o'clock in the afternoon. After morning service, we would go home or head to the basement of the church and eat a hearty dinner of oxtail, rice and peas, green bananas, and yams. Then we would return to church, upstairs, for six o'clock service that wouldn't end until eight thirty or nine o'clock at night. The expectation for a child of six was to remain awake and receive the word of God, or else fire and brimstone would be their resting place. I didn't want to burn forever in hell, so I desperately attempted to stay awake the best I could, but I just couldn't, especially after eating such a healthy meal. Aunt Louise however found a solution to that, and that solution was to pinch me awake—*hard*. Her pinches were not just to awaken me but also a reminder. She would leave bruises and welts on my legs and sides because of how hard she would twist and pinch my skin. When we would return home from a long day of "worshipping," I would get a beating and a stern talking to on the importance of staying awake and "learning your lessons." A few times, Uncle Eddie had to step in and block her rod because she wouldn't stop *teaching me lessons*. But that wasn't unusual, unfortunately; most of the time, no one came to my rescue after suffering periods of relentless beatings. Neither Cleave nor Terrance ever came to help me. I think this was because they feared their mother as much as I did. Uncle Eddie would work long hours and was seldom home during these disciplinary moments, so he also could not help.

I remember getting one beating on a particular Saturday afternoon. I was home alone, and Aunt Louise and Uncle Eddie were out food shopping. Cleave and Terrance also were out doing what they did on a Saturday. I remember I was told *not* to go outside and *not* to turn the television on. Well after a few hours when no one returned home, I got restless and wondered into the front room of my aunt's home. The front room was the "good room" for guests and where the good furniture was—just like the good furniture I knew about from the apartment where my mom, sis, and I lived those early years.

"A television, plastic coverings for the couch, curtains? This is good," I would say to myself.

So, I turned on the television and began to watch a cowboy movie. Cowboy and "Indian" movies were the best. This was the first time I was introduced to John Wayne, Elvis Presley, and other American cinema icons. After watching the cowboy and Indian movie for a while, I heard the car pull up in front of the home. I quickly jumped up to turn the off the TV and run into the hallway. I must have had that same look on my face that my mother saw a few years earlier when I nearly burned the house down. Aunt Louise immediately knew something was wrong just from the expression on my face. As she called me over to help with the groceries, she went into the front room, looked around then went towards the TV and reached behind the Tube Television. It was warm! She came out of the room and smacked me across my face and commenced to beat me after asking Uncle Eddie for his belt. I believe Uncle Eddie hesitated to give it to her a few times, but he must have seen the rage in her eyes from my disobedience and eventually gave in. There were incidents like this all the time where I would be beaten with a belt—which left welts—

and I would believe that I deserved it because I didn't do "as the Lord wanted me to do," so this was my "just reward." However, there came a time when I realized something was wrong. I wasn't going out to play as much; I was getting into fights at school and even began to wet the bed at times. I was not the happy child that would play his Beatles guitar or play with his racing track. As a matter of fact, I don't recall receiving Christmas gifts while living with Aunt Louise, like toys and things a six- or seven-year-old boy might like. I do remember getting clothes from my mother that said "Made in the USA" on the collar, which made me happy—put me in a different place for that moment—as well as put a smile on my face. I knew my mom was still thinking about me and I was hoping to see her soon. But I wasn't the same child. The one incident that really moved me from one place as a child to another was this:

The constant trauma and fear I felt led to my inability to hold my urine at night. A white porcelain bedpan was placed under my bed. I say "the bed" because I shared the bed with Cleave. The bedpan was for me because of my new wetting issues and it was to help me relieve myself without leaving the room and going down the hallway. A few times I admit I had to be reminded to empty the bedpan, because I didn't believe I used it. This one time I recall being called into my bedroom where I shared the bed with cousin Cleve and was asked why I didn't empty the pan. I said I did empty the pan, because I knew I hadn't used it that night. Well, that was an awakening, because the pan was full of urine and now I was responsible for emptying it. I also had to learn a lesson for being disobedient, again, by receiving another beating. By now, beatings had become a common experience in the home for me. No matter what day of the week it was, I would receive some sort of discipline for being disobedient. This last example was what changed me forever, I believe, and placed rage and anger in my heart that I would use against others who were out to hurt me in the future.

After the beating for not emptying the urine filled porcelain bedpan, my aunt called me over to her. At this point I was crying in the corner like most children do when trying to avoid the "wrath of God."

She said, "Get a cup, fill it up, and drink it." I must not have moved right away because she said it again: "Get a cup, fill it up, and drink it."

I hesitantly made my way to the kitchen and got a cup. I could hear her yelling how disobedient I was and that I needed to hurry up or she would "give me something to cry about." I returned to the bedroom and dipped the cup into the white porcelain bedpan that held the yellow urine. I held the cup in my hand, as the overwhelming smell of urine filled my nostrils—which may have been in the pan for a day or two. I gagged at what was about to happen and was at the verge of vomiting. She quickly demanded that I drink the urine to learn my lesson. She threatened to beat me more if I didn't hurry up and drink, so I put the cup to my mouth and drank. She didn't force me to drink it all, but after a few gulps, she beat me to bed. I still remember the smell of that day, in that room with that woman. Aunt Louise still haunts me. That experience hardened me into a walking time bomb—a mentally-sensitive person whose personality and patience sat on opposite ends of the spectrum. Although I might smile when someone would first meet me, underneath lied a sensitive, emotionally-unstable little boy who only wanted to experience the love, smile, and touch of his mother. I would remain in that house with my family for another year. My mother came back to visit once in those three years that we were away from each other, and I grew depressed when I knew she was leaving again.

I cried when she left, but she said, "Next time I see you, Patrick, you'll be with me."

I couldn't wait. For the rest of the time there, things were the same. Beatings, church, good food, pictures with Uncle Eddie, and cowboys and Indians. All these experiences became the norm. It must have been early in 1974 when my uncle and aunt told me that I would be leaving and moving to America to be with my mother. The sudden relief of hearing the possibility that I would be seeing my mother again brought joy and comfort to my soul. So, in August of 1974, I got all dressed up in my plaid red-striped pants and the brown turtleneck sweater that my mother had sent over months before and headed to Heathrow Airport with Uncle Eddie in anticipation of landing at John F. Kennedy Airport in New York.

America, here I come!

Chapter Three

Coming to America

The only thing I ever knew about America was what I saw on television. The shows I grew up watching were being played on the black and white TV in the front room. Cowboy and Indian movies, Elvis Presley specials, John Wayne, Johnny Cash, and the Ten Commandments movie with Charlton Heston were the usual American shows I watched. What good Pentecostal church would not play the movie showing the "Power of God?" The anxiousness of coming to America was overwhelming for so many reasons. First, I would finally be with my mother and that would alleviate the torture and dismay of living under the roof of Aunt Lou. Second, I got to live in the country where my mom went to build a better life, where everything was better for *all* people. A person could become rich or just live a good life in America and that's where my mother was. Third, the American clothes were the best and to top it off, I was going to America where the cowboys and Indians were. America would be the place with much sunshine, lots of money, nice clothes, John Wayne, and fun. Momentarily, my inner smile and laughter would return, and that happy child bounced back.

In August of 1974, at the age of eight and a half, I was put on a flight to John F. Kennedy Airport in New York. I was anxious and excited to get to America. I flew alone but was supervised by the BOAC flight attendant and crew. I was even given my replica flying wings as part of my air travel experience. Americans are nice, I thought—not a bad start as the plane took off into the friendly skies. I remember sitting next to a big Caucasian man who was quite pleasant to me, trying to hold a conversation with me to possibly reduce my fright. Little did he know I wasn't afraid—I was excited! As I sat there listening to him, I observed and listened for the first time the voice and articulation of an American. He had a drawl and an inflection in his voice that was different from the sounds of an English man. I watched many cowboy and Indian movies with John Wayne, and this man sounded a little like him. I also used to mimic John Wayne's voice as I sat in the front room on those days when I was allowed to (and the days I was not) and to my thinking, I believed I was pretty good.

So, as I sat there, the Caucasian man turned to me and asked me a question, "Are you okay?"

This was my first opportunity to "voice" my response. "I'm fine, thank you," I said in my best John Wayne and American impression. Now I don't know what it sounded like to him, but to me I sounded like an American that I saw on television. As I look back, my sense is that it was more of a southern, South Carolina, or even Texas variation. I wondered what he would think of me. Would he call me out? Was he thinking that this kid is doing a terrible job mimicking the American voice? Or this kid sounds weird; do all English people talk this way? Whatever he was thinking, he didn't show any discourse or humor, which was a relief. We talked sporadically through out the ten-hour flight, which kept me up and aware. As we approached New York, the flight attendant said look out your window and see the Statue of Liberty. I never saw it before, neither in pictures nor in movies, but seeing the statue sent chills throughout my body informing me that I had arrived in America. All the pain I experienced in England would be a distant memory, and now, I would be able to live out my life as an American; and there in the Hudson Bay stood the symbol to prove it.

The plane landed at JFK on a hot August day in 1974. I remember it being hot because I was wearing a long-sleeved, brown wool turtleneck sweater, but I didn't feel the heat of the sun because I was too anxious to see my mother. The flight attendant came and got me from my seat and walked me out to the arriving flight terminal where my mother was waiting. She was happy to see me too, with big smiles, hugs, and kisses.

My mother didn't drive at the time, so we took the airport shuttle from NYC to New Rochelle, New York. As we drove along I95, I was amazed how everything in America was so big. The cars were big, the buildings were big (skyscrapers), and so many people. The shuttle arrived at the train station in the town of New Rochelle and immediately I realized the difference in the trains in America, too. The trains in England were managed by a conductor who would close the door for you once you were on and lead you to your seats from what I recall; but here in America, the train doors closed by themselves. *Wow!* I thought. We then took a taxi from the train station to our home, which was also different. In England, the taxis are all black and the same model, but in New Rochelle they were black, blue, or red. We took the black one called Deluxe Taxi to my new home in America. We drove to 140 Washington Avenue in New Rochelle, New York. The house sat on the corner next to a gas station and across from a convenience store that reminded me of the corner store that was across from our home in England where I would go buy my footballs. It was a two-family house, which appeared bigger than the home I had lived in in England. As my mother opened the door and led me up the stairs to her apartment, I was excited to see what home-filled riches my mother had established for my arrival. She then opened our apartment door as she led me directly through to another door that opened up into a bright living space. In the room was an eating table, a bed, a television, and a closet space.

My mother closed the door behind her and said, "This is home."

I was a little confused because from the outside it appeared there were more rooms in the house, but I soon realized we lived in only one of them. My mother explained to me that this is all she could afford right now and that the rest of the house belonged to Ms. Brown. Ms. Brown was an elderly black woman that rented the room to my mother as she worked to establish herself and bring me to the United States. Now that I was here, my mother had to work longer and more often to get a bigger place for us, which meant she had to leave me alone in the house while she was out. Ms. Brown's room was steps away, so my mother entrusted me to her care while she was gone. The first line of business was to get me ready for school, which was to begin in only a few weeks. I attended the elementary school up the hill on Washington Avenue named after the explorer Christopher Columbus. Columbus School was located on the West Side of New Rochelle, where the ethnic makeup was ninety percent Italian and ten percent of ethnicities including black, Mexican, and European. I entered the fourth grade in September wearing my new American clothes and shoes. I was new to the school and so had no established friends. I was nervous but at the same time excited to meet American kids. The first children I met were Louis and Frankie. We called Louis the "Big Greek." He was a handsome kid with the best hair and a good athlete. Later, he was the only white guy on the basketball team who started. Frankie was a quick, witty small kid and a fast talker who was always getting into something. I remember Frankie because his dad drove the big Mayflower moving truck. I had never seen a truck that size before with eighteen wheels! America was big, and the Mayflower moving truck was the perfect example of America's grandeur from the eyes of an English boy who looked at America as the place of great possibilities and big dreams.

The next two people I met were the most significant friends of my childhood (who remain my friends to this day). Kenny "Icky" Bond and Earl Bradshaw. "Icky" was the third kid I met at Columbus School. He lived on the north side but his mother would drive him to school everyday. He was a stocky kid with great agility for his size and could play all the sports. He and I would jump off the hill in the playground while playing tag or Bruce Lee fighting. I knew nothing about Bruce Lee at this time, but I was quickly introduced to him through my friend, Icky. Earl Bradshaw was from the west side, and now I say to him that he was a little schizophrenic with me growing up. Earl was from a hard, middle-class working family that was trying to make it. Earl was also the fastest kid I ever saw run. He always had a smile on his face, even when he was bullying me around.

One day, some kids were trying to bully me and Earl came to my aid and told the kids to leave me alone and that I was "cool." I was cool because I was pretty fast and could play kickball. It became apparent that if you could play sports, you would be accepted and welcomed to play in schoolyard games. I realized early that winning and surrounding yourself with winners was the objective in spite of color or culture. Icky introduced me to baseball where I played softball for Boys Club at the West Side Branch. On the baseball diamond, I learned skills of running, catching, and sliding. I became very good at softball (baseball), and I played for the Boys Club for the next three years. That first year of school was also the start of me learning to fight. Earl had come to my aid once before when I was being bullied as the new kid in the school, but he wasn't always that supportive. He was also there when some "brothers" from the neighborhood wanted to try me and pick on me. I was attacked and smacked around. I tried to defend myself, but I didn't know how. Eventually, they gave up by chasing me home crying. Earl was there, but didn't say anything this time. I'm assuming these were his friends from the "neighborhood" and he didn't want to show allegiance with me over them. One day after a softball game, I was threatened again and chased home. The few times I attempted to protect myself in these fights, I would end up being suspended from school, which meant I would be home by myself or my mom would have to stay home with me and miss work. Because of our economic situation, the latter was not an option. My mother sat me down one day and laid the law down.

She said, "Don't come home again crying that someone beat you up. Fight back—pick up a brick and smash their heads with it!" My mother's statement shocked me because although my time with her in this life was minimal, I never witnessed or heard a negative word come out of her mouth up to that point. The conviction, in which she said those words, shook me more than any words mouthed by my minor attackers. I kept that thought in my mind as I journeyed into the ball fields and hallways of Columbus School. I had many fights my first two years at Columbus School but by the sixth grade I had earned respect from both my male and female peers, as well as my teachers. Dr. Popolardo was the school principal at the time, an Italian man, with olive skin and a constant smile. He was very supportive of me, even when I was getting into fights and he was forced to suspend me. I believe he could have suspended me more if he really wanted to, but he recognized I was different from the other kids and I was an easy target. I was different from the other kids because I was tall, dark, and spoke funny. I spoke the Queen's English. No matter how hard I tried to sound "American," my physical attributes and articulation of words made me stand out amongst the rest of the kids at school, and that made me a target.

At the end of fifth grade, Mr. Popalado came to me and wrote in my black and white composition book: "Great job, Patrick, and I hope to see you in the NFL." I had played a little football on the playground with Icky, Earl, and Louis, but I never thought of playing in the NFL. Actually, I wasn't sure what he was talking about. I had never seen an NFL game before. My only inclination of the game was playing catch in the Columbus School playground during recess. He was the first person to recognize and acknowledge my athletic ability and placed in my head my ability to do more with it. Then, one Sunday, as I recall, I was home watching TV and started channel surfing. I came across an actual American football game. My first impression was that the ball was not the same as the football or Rugby ball used in England, and the size of the players was different too. It was the Super bowl of 1975, the Pittsburgh Steelers versus the Dallas Cowboys. The only play I remember from that game was the acrobatic catch made by Lynn Swann. It was on that day, when that catch became buried in my memory bank, that it moved me to want to know more about this American game called "football." When I returned to school that Monday, I asked Earl and Icky about the game and if they saw it. They said they saw it too and acknowledged that was a great catch confirming that my assessment of the catch was consistent with what others saw on that Sunday afternoon. I told Earl I wanted to play football too. He laughed at first, but said he played football and that he would let me know when the season would start next year and when tryouts would be held.

Entering the sixth grade was a turning point in my life; it was the last year of elementary school and I would be heading to junior high school. As always on the first day back to school, everyone was happy to see each other. Mom and I had moved over the summer to the Lower North Side to North Avenue, which meant I would have a longer walk to school in the mornings. Luckily for me, Icky's Mom (Aunt Jackie) would drive to the bank on Mondays and Wednesdays, so if I got to the bank early enough, I could jump in the orange Volkswagen Bug she drove and get a ride to school. When I saw Earl, I reminded him of his promise to let me know when tryouts were for football. I told him I really wanted to play and asked him not to forget.

He looked at me as though he was going to snap, but he didn't and smiled, "I will, Pat. I won't forget."

Columbus School had an after-school program for kids to learn boxing, basketball, and other games as well as to do homework. One day while I was playing basketball, I saw Earl walk into the gym with a helmet and shoulder pads draped with a red jersey.

I asked him, "What's that?"

He said it was his football equipment. My heart fell. I carefully reminded him that I wanted to play and that he was supposed to let me know where and when tryouts were. With as much remorse as a ten-year old could have, he said he was sorry and that he forgot. That was a downer. I would have to wait an entire year before I would have a chance to put on the pads.

Seventh grade was a different story. I attended this big, stone-castle-looking-school located on the Lower East Side of New Rochelle: Isaac E. Young. Isaac was a good time in my adolescent years; I made a lot of friends and learned a lot about Italians. Many of my Italian friends who went to Columbus went to Isaac. There was one thing about the Italian kids I knew: there was no question about their manhood and commitment to their community. There are too many of them to list here but I want to give a big shout out to West Side Italian Boys. Many of them played with me in the school grounds and welcomed me into their lives. The next important event was when Earl came and provided the date and time of the tryouts for the Chiefs.

I asked, "What's that?"

As I took the permission slip from his hands. He said, "It's the name of the team you and I will play on this year." He said, "Ask for Mr. Flowers or Mr. Bailey and don't be late." He emphasized, "Don't be late."

I was excited to attend the signups for the Chiefs. On signup day, right after school I walked from the West Side of New Rochelle to the East Side of New Rochelle. I walked to New Rochelle High School where the signups were being held on the grass field in front of the school. I asked for Mr. Flowers and another adult directed me to him. Mr. Flowers was a big man. Not fat, not burly, but well-built and put together for an older man. He was a detective in the city of New Rochelle and a well-loved man. The park where we would play our games was later named in honor of him and his service to the youth of the city. I was given the necessary paperwork to bring home for my mother to sign and my name was put on the list. I was told to report to practice the next day: *Don't be late, or you'll be running extra lakes.*

I didn't know what that meant, but I would soon find out.

The next day came and I got to practice on time. Practice was held in the front of the high school. The field was divided to accommodate the three teams: Redskins, Thunderbolts, and Chiefs. As eleven-year-olds waited for the coaches to appear, I observed how everyone knew one another. The only person I recognized was Earl. Icky was playing at this time as well, but he was much bigger than most of us and moved to the team with the bigger kids: the Colts. Within minutes after getting there, I saw Mr. Flowers walking up the walkway with two other men by his side. One had a walkie talkie and the other had a notebook. Neither of them smiled then and they never smiled for the entire season. Mr. Bailey carried the notebook. He was the black history teacher in the high school. The other man was Mr. Holly—a no nonsense Mount Vernon Police detective. I wasn't sure if I wanted to play this game of football anymore if the coaches looked like this. I must admit I was scared—scared before I knew anything about football, needless to say not knowing how to win at this level. After introductions and the collection of permission slips, we were all directed to take a "lap." I looked around and all the kids jumped to their feet and started running towards the lakes.

"When in Rome, do as the Romans do." So, I followed.

A lap was a warm-up, an-under-four-minute-jog around the two manmade lakes in front of the high school. Put together they measured one-quarter of a mile or so long. The jog was more like a sprint because the coaches would watch to see who was lagging or taking their time. I would usually come in at the front of the pack. Jim Yacone usually came in first. (Jim later went to West Point. His story is told in the book, "Black Hawk Down.") The practices were tough and dirty, but I learned to tackle, to run faster, and tackle harder. I asked myself, How was I able to do this? I realized that while I was tackling, I had a sense anger coming from within and a high level of intensity while tackling. I would exert a moment of rage while the play was going on and I didn't know why. Before the first game of my first Pee Wee Junior Midget team, I was named the right starting defensive end. My basic responsibilities were to get to the quarterback and make sure no one got around me. Mr. Bailey, Mr. Holly, Mr. Flowers, and Joe Fosina, who took care of much of the managing of the teams and ensuring the administration of the team was in place, made me into the player and man I am today. I am thankful for them and everything they taught me.

There were possibly many incidents like this while on the Chiefs, but this particular event sticks in my mind to this day. It's funny now when I talk to Earl and Icky about those events forty years ago, but it was no laughing matter at the time. The Chiefs were on our way back from a game and, as usual, we won. That year we went undefeated and un-scored upon. On our way home, I remember sitting up front and most of the neighborhood guys were in the back row of seats making joyful celebratory cheers after winning. Suddenly, out of nowhere, Mr. Holly's walkie talkie went flying in the air towards the back of the bus, followed with "Shut the f—— up!" The bus went dead silent. Mr. Holly was our defensive coach; he was demanding but a great teacher as well. He expected you to follow and replicate what he showed you. He made you a better person whether you wanted to be or not. The lesson learned that day was not to take for granted your short-term successes, for until the job is complete you must stay focused to the end. Mr. Holly and Mr. Bailey taught me through sports what it takes to be successful in America: hard work, dedication, and focus. This would be my first and only season playing for the Pop Warner Chiefs, but it wouldn't be the last where I would be coached or interacting with at least one of these great men of New Rochelle. At the close of the season there was a banquet dinner. My mother couldn't attend because she had to work. That night as they called out the awards, the coaches would call out both the Offensive and Defensive MVPs of the season. Out of the eleven players on defense, and the great, hard-hitting, fast players like Earl Bradshaw and running back, Rick Anderson—who were on my team—I never thought I would get an award separate from the team participation trophy.

Then the Defensive MVP's name was called: "Patrick Morrison, Most Valuable Defensive Player."

I sat there and looked around in shock that my name had been called. Did I hear right? My ears went dead because I didn't hear the clapping or yelling of my teammates telling me to go up and get my trophy. My head cleared a few minutes later as I got up and received my first award for playing this game I grew to love. This was 1978. I had been in America for only four years and wasn't sure what my future would be or what I sounded like. I don't think it really mattered anymore because now I was an American football player, and a good one at that!

Chapter Four

The Grid Iron

I was thirteen going on fourteen-years-old and about to enter the ninth grade. Isaac E. Young Middle School had a football team, so many of us who were from West Side or Lower North Side went to this school and also went out for the football team. We had a good team: the Italian guys from the West Side and the fellas from the South Side. I don't remember our record that year, but I do remember the outcome of one particular game—the game against our school's rival, Albert Leonard. Albert Leonard was located in the Northeast section of the city. The school was culturally and economically diverse like Isaac, which allowed the student athletes to concentrate on the competition and not on color or ethnicity. The new demographics of the team provided a sense of cohesiveness—which did away with social divisions based on economics, race, haves, and have nots. This special relationship amongst the student athletes provided a platform for success for Albert Leonard over us and others throughout Westchester County Junior High School League.

The cultural personalities that made up Isaac had an effect on me and how to approach the game of football. One particular classmate, that had a profound effect on how to play the game, as well as socially integrating me to the community and sports, was D Rowe. D Rowe was much taller than all of us. I was tall for my age at six feet in the ninth grade, but Daren might have already been 6 4″. He was so much taller than everyone else that his nickname was "Lurch," after the TV character in the sitcom, Adams Family. D Rowe's family was from Panama; he had two older brothers and one younger sister. He was 6 4″ and probably 140 pounds. You may ask the question, how could a boy so tall and weighing so little be playing football and integrating me into the game? He was indifferent. He was indifferent in the way that he didn't care what you thought or who you were. With girls, it was a paradox. He would say to a girl, "Come here." If they refused, he would say, "Didn't you hear me calling you? Get over here." The girl would say no sometimes and keep walking or would come over. If the girl came over, he would say something like "Are you okay? You need anything or is anyone bothering you?" He was a caring dude that had a switch that could be turned on and off quickly.

He and I would fight every year from seventh grade to ninth grade. An example of the switch would come frequently when he didn't want to be called Lurch. Some days it wouldn't bother him and other days it would bring on a physical confrontation that would warrant intervention. He and I fought fist-to-fist and cuff-to-cuff yearly, but after every fight we made up and moved on. I stole his approach to the world and his interaction with everyone around him—which he also instituted on the field. D, at 140 pounds, played defensive end, and his ability to play effectively and cause havoc at the position was something to behold. He actually would knock kids out of the game at least three times within a season. His level of viciousness is what I took note of and applied it to my game. It seemed like he played with anger and a sense of demand. I don't know if his approach to the game was due to hardships from his homeland or more from being an immigrant from a poor country whose family had to work hard and fight to get to America, a guy who wasn't going to let anything get in his way of achieving the American dream. I don't know the source of his fury. D had previously played football on the Chiefs with me and that is where I first witnessed his brutality on the field; so, I was surprised when I received the MVP the year earlier. Was I mimicking the way to play the game from watching D and without even knowing it? Where did my anger come from? Was it from my experience with Aunt Louise? My mother leaving me? D Rowe? I don't know, but in retrospect, I thank D Rowe for showing me what it took to be successful on the gridiron— which was to show tenacity, audacity, and passion for the game. I believe D Rowe played two seasons of high football and then concentrated on basketball. His basketball career later took off: he became a New Rochelle High School Hall of Famer and went on to play Division I college basketball, eventually playing many years in Europe where he was an MVP. After his career, he returned to the United States and utilized his experience and expertise on the college coaching level. It's men like D Rowe that showed me some basic elements of how to be successful in American sports and life. Making it in America is not an easy task, nor is it an easy place to live, but it is a place where dreams do come true.

So, in the ninth grade, those remaining players from the Pop Warner days who attended Isaac Young knew of the rivalry between the two schools. Isaac had the neighborhood kids mostly and some Pop Warner players, such as Stuffy—a short-in-stature, great athlete with a body of a Greek god—Nicky P., John T., Icky, and T.D. Albert Leonard, because of its location to the high school and Pop Warner practice area, had more Pop Warner players, coupled with the surrounding neighborhood children. The big rivalry game was at hand and I remember the names of the participants like it was yesterday. They were already superstars in junior high school who were looked upon as the future high school and potential college stars. They had names like "Slick Rick"—who had moves, quickness, and speed that was unmatched as a junior high school runner. There was Philip, a smooth, tall, athletically-built running back who shared the backfield with Slick Rick. Then you had Dion, a Jamaican track speedster who was built like a racehorse. Then there were the linemen; those that know football know it's the big boys up front on the defensive and offensive lines that make the difference. The offensive line consisted of Jim M., Hubert P., Alvin, and Big B. For the reader to get a better perspective of the Albert Leonard offensive line, Big B was 6′9″, 308 pounds in 8th grade, and later recruited to the University of Maryland. Jim M. was later recruited to play offensive line for Nebraska, and Alvin went to Duke University. As soon as the game began, I knew we were in trouble. Slick Rick returned the kickoff to our twenty-yard line within seconds of the start of the game. Throughout the game, I realized that to play this game at the next level (high school) I would have to do better; if not, I would not see the field at all. We were crushed by Albert Leonard that day. Richard D., "Biggie," and additional Albert Leonard linemen stars shut down any running game we had; and our only "it" factor, Stuffy B, could not get loose and was shut down too. We had no one to compete with the massive bodies of Albert Leonard. I realized it would take something else to win at this game. Yes, size, but those guys brought something else to the game. Today, we call it "swagger." They had swagger, and they knew they had it, as well as the manpower to win. They were unquestionably arrogant, and rightfully so, because they eventually went undefeated for the rest of the season. Swagger—I never had it. I was still trying to learn the game. I didn't have long, established, and organic relationships with family and the community. I didn't have a sense of comradeship rooted in the neighborhood, which would naturally develop a sense of purpose and confidence. I still felt like an outsider trying to establish myself in the community to gain respect from my peers.

Playing Pop Warner and for Isaac taught me a lot about American life and its relationship to athletics. I recognized that football could be the way out of a particular social class. It opened up opportunities for players to provide a better future for their families. At that time, when you would see Ricky run, you knew he would go on to college to play; when you saw Ben, Dickson, or Mckean, you knew they would have opportunities to do the same. So, I, too, thought that about myself. I wanted to be like them—to be known, recognized—to have the opportunity to relieve the burden off my mother who was struggling to provide for me and my little brother, who had just been born a few years earlier.

I played basketball as well, but as I reflect back on that period, I shouldn't have. I wanted to play because at that point Clive had become a basketball superstar in the area, state, and was one of the best players in the country. Sports were helping the family assimilate and helping us move forward in the land of opportunity. I played because he was my cousin and I thought I could be like him. I worked hard; I could jump, and I was aggressive. The problem was, I couldn't shoot like him—and I could not shoot consistently at all. I hadn't devoted time to the game like I did in football and like he did in basketball. Basketball helped me with learning a game and different skillsets that made me more agile and patient. I played football with aggression. However, with basketball, more patience, less aggression, and finesse were needed to reach success on the court. Up to this point, the deference of how to play in the two sports was foreign to me and the techniques and strategies were totally different. I later realized that my decision to continue playing basketball was a disservice to my future endeavors and myself. I came to this realization as the school year ended in ninth grade as I was heading to the big school, New Rochelle High, to begin a new chapter in my immigrant student-athlete life.

Every Thanksgiving Day in New Rochelle back in the late '70s and early '80s, Westchester County, as well as parts of NYC, would wake up and turn on their TV to watch the annual Thanksgiving Day parades. We would also watch the big football game televised throughout the tri-state area on Channel 11 between New Rochelle High and its rival—Catholic school powerhouse—Iona Prep. Iona Prep was located approximately two miles up the road from New Rochelle High School in a picturesque suburban neighborhood. Iona was a private school, so we at New Rochelle High always looked at that as the place for privileged kids who lived good, stress-free lives absent from gangs and drugs. That experience was a sharp contrast to the majority of students of "New Ro" who came from blue-collar families, white-collar workers, and welfare, with varied issues including gangs and drugs. This was the big game of the year to determine best team in the area. It was also a time to watch the big boys from the high school that as a Pop Warner kid one would hear about in the papers or on television. The names for New Rochelle were legendary, such as A Rowe, linebacker; he was D Rowe's older brother, who we later referred to as our Lawrence Taylor. There was also Sonny Fernandez, Michael W., and Kyle G.—who came from a family of New Rochelle sport heroes and high school All-Americans. "LC" Corn also started in New Ro and went on to become the first black quarterback at the University of Connecticut. There were many more players that I can't recall right now, but they were all coached by a former New Rochelle High standout and legend, Harold Crocker.

This year was my first year at New Rochelle High and I continued playing football on the JV team. The team now consisted of IEY and Albert Leonard players. One of the wonderful things about New Rochelle was the city was small enough in square miles that most people knew each other's family or had friends of other friends that knew each other. That reduced some of the battles in the school, mainly because of family ties throughout the city. The team was made up of Albert Leonard guys who from the previous year had beat up on us pretty bad at Isaac Young, and, of course, the fellas from IEY: me, Icky, Earl, T.D., and Nunzio. We were coached again by Mr. Bailey, who had recently been given the position of JV coach at the high school. We were happy to have him coach the JV team because many of us were coached by him a few years earlier while playing on the Chiefs and we knew what to expect. It was a welcome delight. Even though Mr. Bailey was tough on us, he made us better players and better people because he didn't believe in excuses, just outcomes. He worked us hard in the classroom as well as on the football field. Under Coach Bailey's tutelage, the JV team went undefeated. This was a great accomplishment, but no one really cared about JV, they were more concerned with Varsity and the players that dominated the headlines up there. We knew we were the best in Westchester County and we were aiming to let everyone know for the rest of our high school careers that we were great and even better than the current varsity team. There was another eye-opening situation that revealed something about playing this game and that was the makeup of our team. As I mentioned before, Albert Leonard's team was filled with speed, size, and "swagger." Our team was made up of hard working, good athletes that just played the game the way we were taught. When we got to the high school, the JV team took on a new distinct personality. The defense was not occupied with Albert Leonard players and neither was the offense. On defense, the two middle linebackers were Icky and T.D. Earl played safety. Nunzio played nose tackle. Rob Castags, (another IEY lineman) played defensive tackle with me at defensive end and Stuffy at quarterback and running back. We started at the most crucial positions on the field. At that time, Albert Leonard guys played the finesse positions: running back, wide receiver—mostly offense. It takes a particular mindset to play defense, a particular attitude and a particular inner intensity, most of which was rewarded the following year.

This first year at the high school was an exciting one! JV was undefeated and so was varsity. Varsity had its state championship game held at Memorial Field in Mount Vernon, New York, the neighboring town to New Rochelle (which was also a rival of ours and not such a pleasant, friendly rivalry at that). The game would bring in local and national news coverage, as well as an opportunity for all the communities to come out and watch great football between two great cities and programs. I remember standing with Icky, Fudge, and Hubert—who played tight end and the other defensive end (from Albert Leonard)—along the fence that separated the field from the fans. To watch the varsity players play was like watching the Pittsburgh Steelers play that Sunday afternoon in 1975. Kyle G would stretch forth and reach up and make incredible catches in the middle of defenders from throws tightly spun by LC, and it was as pretty as Terry Bradshaw throwing a touchdown to Lynn Swann. It was amazing to watch these young men play the game with so much focus and determination and teamwork. I realize they were not only great high school football players, but were friends too. Sports are an activity that brings youth from all over the city, from different socioeconomic backgrounds, to a common place to achieve the common goal of winning.

The most recognized player on that team from my perspective was A. Rowe. He was the Jack Lambert of New Rochelle. He looked like L.T. He stood about 6 3″ and weighed 215 pounds. He wore the number "58" and played middle linebacker. Remember, he was one of the older brothers of D. Rowe from Panama. I looked at him as a player who came from a foreign country and could make it to the NFL. In this championship game against Kingston High, a powerhouse from upstate New York, A. Rowe made one of the most incredible and amazing plays that anyone would want to see. Throughout the game it was a battle between New Ro and Kingston. This would not be a pushover win for New Ro by any stretch of the imagination; but when it came down to the fourth quarter, Kingston was threatening to score with a fourth down, less than twenty seconds to play in the game, and the ball was on the one-yard line. It didn't look good for New Ro, even though New Ro had shown its dominance throughout the year and had demonstrated its ability to compete in this game. It appeared too much to ask for with such little time to stop the inevitable. The ball was snapped, and Kingston decided on a running play off the tackle hole. As I stood there next to Icky and Hubert along the chained fence, my heart stopped, and it appeared that time stood still as we watched the play unfold before us. As the running back approached the line of scrimmage and attempted to leap into the end zone and end the game, we watched the athletic ability, tenacity, and commitment to stopping the play by this one person. It was as if we were watching Jack Lambert up close, stopping Preston Pearson, and raising havoc in the Dallas Cowboys backfield. A. Rowe timed his jump at the very moment the running back ascended towards the line and met him in the air for a collision that sent him backwards, never crossing the end zone. A Rowe had stopped Kingston's running back just as time expired. To witness 15,000 people screaming in joy within the midst of moans of defeat was the paradox of an experience. That one play changed everything for New Ro High and my outlook on the game. I learned that at any moment your "number" can be called upon, and I wondered if I would be ready to answer that call. On that night A. Rowe was ready, and within two years, my number would be called too, and I would have to answer the call.

After a year in high school, I found my self fully integrated and assimilated to the culture. My first real relationship was with Darci. Darci came from a middle-class family and was one of five sisters. By now I had come to be known as Pat Morrison, the tall dark football player. And I must admit I had a few admirers. Darci was on the cheerleading team, which had some of the best looking young ladies in Westchester, beautiful and smart. I mention Darci because during the time of my junior year, many of my friends started to run into personal issues and slowly, one by one, began to leave my circle of friends, the first of them being Philip. Philip was the outstanding running back from Albert Leonard who involved himself in activities which consequently led to many run-ins with the law. To top it off, he didn't participate in school at a rate he needed to. He later left school and consequently stopped playing football. The next person was Dion H. Not sure why he stopped playing. It may have been because his playing time was reduced due to the multiple impact players we had in the backfield. Darci let me go and decided with one of her girlfriends to begin hanging around the guys from another school, which also caused disruption in their lives. I didn't know the details; all I knew was my friends were falling away. It was the beginning of a difficult year as a student athlete. My junior year, New Rochelle had just come off a year being named state champions. A.Rowe had graduated and was offered to play football at Wagner College in LI, where he was selected All-American his freshman year. Michael W., the state champion running back, and Sonny, the state champion defensive back, went on to Southern Connecticut under the coach Kevin Gilbride. L.C., who orchestrated the state championship offense, went on to the University of Connecticut where he started. And there were others like "Bill Hill" who went on to Syracuse and played defensive end. So many players made up that team which demonstrated the will and example of how to win. But my junior year wouldn't be so successful. Now we were made up of juniors and a few seniors—some seniors who had played the year before and some who had not. We went into the season with high hopes, but unfortunately it didn't turn out that way. One particular game stands out in my mind and as it has had a lasting effect on my teammates and me to this day; it we would not soon forget. It was a game against Roosevelt High School, in Yonkers, New York. Tony Demateo, a legend in Yonkers, along with his brother, Donny, coached the team. Players from New Rochelle and Yonkers never got along. The two cities would frequently clash at parties and events around Westchester frequently, and many times this animosity would resurface at sporting events. Our junior year, Roosevelt was beating us badly. Our offense couldn't move the ball and their manpower out muscled us. The thing about this game that was so unsettling was the fact that in the fourth quarter, they were beating us 21-0 and were still trying to score more touchdowns with less than five minutes left in the game. Within the last three minutes there was a fumbled ball and I was able to pick it up and score a touchdown. That was the highlight of the game for us, because after that Roosevelt went on full blitz and scored two more touchdowns beating us 36-6. That was the most humiliating loss most of us had ever felt. We were embarrassed and felt disappointed for the seniors because it was as though the younger players weren't able to live up to what was expected of us as New Ro football players. That day many of us cried. Under Mr. Bailey, Mr. Holly, and Mr. Flowers we had never suffered a loss and didn't expect anything like this to happen. To have now experienced such a bad loss made us feel we let everyone down in New Ro, including the little ones watching us from the sidelines.

My personality remained the same, and I had friends both male and female who respected me. I got along with kids from the block and the projects as well as ones from the north end. One thing about New Rochelle High is that we all got along so well with one another. There were times when I noticed the segregation in the school and the ethnic groups associating among themselves, which was usually during lunchtime. It was obvious, but at the same time appeared normal. The high school had two lunchrooms: one upstairs on the main floor and the other in the lower floor basement. I ate in the upper lunchroom. I remember the first table being occupied by sophomore girls. I recall this because whenever I walked into the lunchroom I could hear the girls whispering amongst themselves, laughing and pointing at me like I was a museum piece. Behind them at the next two tables were usually the upper-class Anglo-Saxon and Jewish kids—kind of rowdy tables, which always consisted of at least one crazy white guy. The table in the far rear was occupied by the West Indian community of students—Jamaican or Caribbean. I never sat with them because I didn't identify with them at the time. At that time in America, people from the islands were still looked upon as *unique* and as outsiders, even though people from the West Indies had been here for many years working and contributing to American society. I didn't want to feel that way; I wanted to be looked upon as a black American. So, whenever someone would ask where I was from, I would say New Rochelle. They would say, "No, where were you born?" It was if they knew from my features or something that I was from a place other than America. Maybe my features, maybe I still had a slight accent—I don't know. I would eventually tell everyone I was born in England and my dad was British. I don't know why I hated to acknowledge that part of me. My mother worked hard to provide for me. Maybe there was something missing in my life that prevented me from acknowledging who I was and who I had become as a man then. I sat with the "brothers." Mitchell B.—we went to Isaac together. He was the cool, popular guy who had money and played basketball and football. He was actually IEY's fullback but stopped playing football when we got to the high school. He wore the latest gear, and everyone loved him. He could even rap. Guys and girls would gather around the lunch table at lunchtime. He would make a beat with hands and rap away with rhymes that would challenge some of the rappers of today.

My years at New Ro opened up and revealed a side of young American culture that I got to understand and experience up close and personal. Icky, Earl, and others were my best friends and they understood me and always introduced me to new things that allowed me to further assimilate to American culture. I had friends and I was in the mix now. Girls liked me. I was a football player and had American friends; but I still felt like I was an outsider. Many of the kids had kinships that ran generations. My history began with my mother and I. Clive had already graduated and went off to college; and Beverly was now a senior and I would go see her at certain times of the day when I knew she was in home economics class in the art section of the school. That's the only time I had free—plus she was a girl and older, so I didn't feel to be hanging around her like that. The younger sister, Valery, went to Mt. Vernon High, so I never saw her around unless we went visiting on a Sunday afternoon. So, although externally things appeared fine, internally I was in a personal turmoil. I was angry all the time and had mood swings.

One day while over at Icky's house hanging out, Icky was playing around and then started roughhousing with me. After telling him to stop a couple of times, I turned around and punched him in the face with my fist. I was shocked, and he was shocked too. He looked at me and said, "Motherf——er, get out of my house before I kick your ass!" Icky was about 5 10″, 220 pounds, and was the linebacker on the football team. He said, "Don't come back, because if you do, I'm going to shoot you." I was scared as s——! He went straight to the gun. Icky's stepfather was a corrections officer and also trained K-9 German shepherds for the department. My first thought was, *Would Icky let me out of the house with his trained K-9 that was constantly on guard, and was he really going to shoot me with a gun I knew nothing about?*

He opened the door and let me out of the house as I made my way home. I think that was the first time where I saw spontaneous anger explode from within me. I didn't speak to Icky for weeks after that. I tried to call and apologize but he didn't want to take my calls or hear any of it. Finally, his mother answered the phone one day one and asked what happened between us. I told her, "I hit Icky in the face, but I didn't mean it." She said I shouldn't let that stop us from being friends; it was a mistake. Well I knew that, but Icky had another position. So, I went over to Icky's—which was across the street from my church—a few Sundays later. He let me in. I hesitated because I wanted to see where the dog was. Sport (that was his dog's name) was looking down the stairs at me, ready for the call to pounce on the dark intruder.

We sat down in the front room as he began, "What the f—— man!"

"I didn't mean it. I was just upset about something and you wouldn't stop. I'm sorry." I asked him, "Were you really going to shoot me?"

He said, "Yes," and said, "Come in my room." We went to his room and sat down on the chair and bed. He went to his closet and pulled out a Western .45 caliber gun, the kind I saw in the old Western movies. He started laughing and said it was a BB gun, which was a relief. He said it hurt though if you got too close. He went on to tell me more about the BB gun and how the air cartridges worked. We never argued again. To this day, Icky is my best friend aside from my wife. He is more like a brother from another mother. My temper began to get the worst of me as time went on. It eventually began to affect my relationship with my mother. I became uncontrollable. I stayed out late at night and I would not call to inform her of my whereabouts. I was absentminded, leaving dinners for my brother and I on the stove and burning them. I even became oppositional and defiant. One day, I was so filled with anger and rage after my mother gave me a good tongue lashing, which only a Jamaican mother can give, that I left the house (at this time we were living in an apartment building with a slum lord). As I stomped out of the house, slamming the room and apartment doors, she said, "Don't come back."

I walked four miles to Mt. Vernon to my cousin's house. I cried and yelled as I walked along East Lincoln Avenue the entire four miles and to bed that night. The next day must have been a Saturday because I went and spoke in detail to my aunt about what happened and told her that my mother had told me not to come back.

Aunt Evelyn, in her comforting and convincing voice told me, "Your mother loves you. When you were born, she was so proud and happy you were here. She loves you. She didn't mean it."

I then spoke to Clive, who was in college. He listened and said, "She was just upset; go home." I didn't go home that day, but my mom called and asked if I was there. She had already called Icky's house and found out that I wasn't there. She told Aunt Evelyn to tell me to come home. So, later that evening, I did and went straight to my room and closed the door. I heard my mom coming down the hallway.

She yelled out my name, "Patrick."

I said, "Yes."

"Okay," she said, and we both went to bed.

My mother later scheduled an appointment with a child counselor to "evaluate and assess" what might be the root cause of my explosive behavior. However, since I was responsible to attend these meetings on my own, I went to two meetings and called it quits. The unfortunate thing about that was the therapist never connected to me from what I remember. He was sterile and bland in his approach, and for a young boy who was active and personable, it would have been a great opportunity for him and me to work together and search out the root cause of my anger. I would soon understand this anger from my own evaluation and assessment, and that much of it derived from feeling empty as an outsider in my own community.

The summer of 1982 was filled with excitement. There were still those lazy summer days when one could sleep in all day or invite friends over to eat and watch TV. We would take turns either going to Icky or T.D.'s house or just staying at mine, making hamburgers and drinking Kool-Aid. Other days I played stickball in the back parking lot on Lawn Avenue with neighborhood kids at the apartment house we lived in before we moved to North Avenue. It was my senior year and there was a lot to prove based on the prior season's disappointing record, but now the team was made up of a majority of seniors and juniors who had played together since Pop Warner days. We were mature and ready to go.

I don't remember all the games, but there are a few which stood out and have not succumbed to time and age, the first being our game against Mamaroneck High School. The town of Mamaroneck is located north of New Rochelle and its population consists of middle to upper middle-class households.

It's an area with good kids, good schools, and good neighborhoods. I remember that game because I brought havoc to their lives on the field that day. I had multiple sacks, tackles, and disruptions in the backfield. Our offense also had a field day running all over them. The second game I remember was against Yonkers High, coached by one of the Demateo brothers. As mentioned earlier, the Demateo brothers were coaching legends in Westchester known for winning games and famous for beating us the year before. They've been known to have great high school players who have gone on to play in Division I programs; so I give him credit for that. The most memorable thing about that game occurred prior to the game starting during our warmups. We would warm-up in the end zone area of our side of the field when playing at home. As we sat on the ground doing our static stretches, the Yonkers football team came up from behind and walked right through the middle of our stretches! I recall I was to the left of them, Earl was up front, Icky was in the middle, and then there was everyone else. It was like a bell had gone off in Earl's head and he went crazy. He yelled at Coach Crocker to do something. It was like Crocker was stunned and couldn't believe it himself.

Earl called off the stretching and told us all to get up while cursing, "F— — these motherf——ers, they will pay."

Icky lost his mind and wanted to run over to them before the kickoff and get the game unofficially started. Me—my head was just in another place. I was angry to the point of being out of control. The blessing of football is that it's a physical sport that provides an outlet for me to release tensions and frustrations when I didn't have the language to express them. That day, none of us had the words to express the anger we had for the disrespect Yonkers showed New Ro football, but our expression on the field spoke loud and clear that the disrespect would not be tolerated in our house on our field. We won that game 38-0. To this day, when I run into former Yonker's players, they say I don't know what we were thinking about that day, and they still remember the names, Sick Icky, Earl Bradshaw, and me. But as bad as that game was for Yonkers and the anger myself and the rest of the team felt, it failed to compare to when we had our rematch with the other Damateo brother from Roosevelt High.

The previous year's game was still fresh in our minds—especially mine. I was still angry from our disappointing loss and embarrassment. The day was a warm, eighty-degree weather day in September. We were feeling good in our purple and gold uniforms with a splash of white on our helmets. The guys were up and ready for revenge as usual. Earl led the chatter by reminding us of what happened the year before. He made it clear to everyone that we better get them back. Funnily enough, it reminded me of when we were back in Columbus School, how Earl would "bully" to make sure you got his point, and then quickly switch it off again. I learned this lesson as I grew into manhood, the importance of "turning it on and off." This game, however, was the time to turn it on, but, unfortunately, we hadn't matured enough to learn to turn it off.

I would say that the beating Roosevelt took this game might have been their worst up to that point in their history. We were so vicious with our tackling and overall presence that I truly believe the Roosevelt players didn't want to play anymore. We knocked a minimum of five players out of the game and were seeking for more. After each play, the referees tried to calm us down and even penalize us, which only made the defense angrier. We would then let loose on them again and send the quarterback or running back to the original line of scrimmage. Our offense was pretty rested for the game because they weren't on the field that much, due to the number of penalties the defense kept getting. Coach Crocker didn't really hold us back. He did recognize that we were a little out of control and had to call a timeout a few times. However, the timeouts were just to allow us to catch our breaths, because every time coach came out, he smiled and asked us if we were okay.

Earl immediately went into, "Coach, I haven't forgot about what they did last year."

Crocker would leave the huddle; the referees would blow the whistle to start the down; and we would commence to "bring the heat" and aim to remind them too.

The last game that left an impact on me and had me assess who I was and how much my actions could affect my future and my mother was when we suffered our only loss of that '82 season. At that time, we were looking to break the school records on defense, go undefeated, and head to the state championship for the second time in three years. To reach that goal, we had to go through another Yonkers team: Gorton. It was the battle of the two top teams in Westchester Division A1, where the winner would head to the state finals in Syracuse, New York. Gorton had one of the top running backs who was heading to Boston College to play the following year. We had both the size and speed to beat them, so we didn't worry much about getting by them. New Ro football was on a roll and we were the captains of the ship. Well, unfortunately, the ship sank, and we lost 12-6. The running backs couldn't get loose, the linebackers weren't getting to the ball like usual, and Gorton was running through our line like it didn't exist. By this time in the season, we were down one or two enforcing players. One was Jim Mc., who decided not to play that season for fear he would hurt himself and not be able to play for Nebraska the upcoming year. After the game we all headed to the bus and took the twenty-minute ride back to New Rochelle from Mt. Vernon City Field. I took my time getting back to the locker room because I was so upset about the loss and I had to calm down before talking to anyone. By then, most of the guys were in the locker room back at the school getting undressed. Suddenly, I heard Coach Crocker heading towards the back row of the lockers where most of the starters' lockers were. Icky's, Earl's, Ben's, Stuffy's, and Biggie's—I heard all the lockers closing and so did coach.

So, Crocker asked, "What happened today and why are all the lockers closing?" He knew something was up. So, he opened up one locker and then another and then another and to his surprise saw alcohol bottles: Ole English 800.

One of the bottles was found in my locker and when asked if it was mine, I said, "No and I don't know how it got in there."

I believe someone spoke up later and told coach that I wasn't back there drinking. That day was a day that changed many of my friends' lives. These guys had taught me how to play the game of football. I wouldn't have been there if it wasn't for them. I knew I felt guilty for not going along with them and taking the blame with them, but what would my mother have thought about her son who she had worked so hard to bring to America, working up to three jobs to keep food on the table and lights on in the house for her family? How could I let her down by being a part of something that could ruin my future? Coach had to make a decision. We had one more game left, the annual Turkey Bowl Thanksgiving game. The same game I watched, and they watched growing up. Our time had come to show the state what New Ro football had to offer and showcase one another's skills against our archrival, Iona Prep. Coach Crocker made probably the hardest decision he had to make in his high school career, either to sit on the latest revelation or follow protocol and suspend the guys for having alcohol on school grounds. He decided on the later, and the suspensions were handed out to my friends. Their dreams of playing in the Turkey Bowl in front of college coaches and their families were washed away. Aunt Jackie, Icky's mom, cried and was angry. Many people thought coach shouldn't have said anything until after the Turkey Bowl Game. I believe coach made that decision to teach us the lesson that principle and accountability outweighs winning a game. I wouldn't have wanted to be in his shoes to make that decision at that time. The event around the suspensions made the local newspaper, The Standard Star, along with the tri-state paper, The Daily News.

As the spectators made their way into Memorial Field in Mount Vernon, one could feel something special in the air. It felt like the clouds had opened up and God had given his special blessing on that day. The day was sunny and bright. There were blue skies, a perfect day for football. Something was missing though: the chatter and the enthusiastic exuberance of Earl getting us ready for the game and the quiet presiding intensity coming from Icky's vicinity. I felt alone without my boys. It was time for me to be the leader and set the example. This was my time to show that I belonged. That day turned out to be the turning point of my football career. Ironically, my teammates, who I considered to be the stars of the team, could have easily obtained the recognition they deserved and the opportunities to play in college that day. Unfortunately for them, but fortunately for me, that opportunity was about to be taken full advantage of. As the crowd roared play-after-play by the plays our defense was making, one could tell it was going to be a special day. We were playing for those guys that were on the sidelines, for ourselves as redemption for our last loss, losing to Iona the year before, and for the New Ro family. I heard later that television announcers were saying that I had wrapped up the MVP award in the first half of the game. I was on a mission—in a zone. I was angry for no apparent reason. I was excited to be in the game and I was disappointed that the rest of the guys weren't playing next to me. In the first half of the game, I brought out all my emotions onto the field. Other than bringing confusion and vicious hits, I had a fumble recovery, blocked punt, and two defensive touchdowns. It was the most impressive game of my career. I don't know if the game would have turned out the same way if all the guys had played, but like I said, there was something special about that day. That day reinforced for me that at any moment and time my number could be called upon and begged the question of whether I would be ready to respond. That day was a good day. I responded. I executed, and we won.

By this time in my football journey, the cultural makeup of the New Rochelle team was limited to a few. There was myself, who was born in London, England; Nunzio, who was born in Italy; and Hubert Parris, who was born in Jamaica. Philip had stopped playing due to off-the-field issues, and Daren was no longer playing football but was in full stride heading towards a collegiate career with basketball. Race and culture never found its way in dividing New Rochelle football players. We didn't allow our race to be defined by others or ourselves. All that we wanted as a collective unit was guys that wanted to play football and carry on the tradition of winning at New Ro and possibly going on to college to play.

Chapter Five

Respect Due

I played the last game of my high school career and had a feeling of relief, but at the same time a feeling of what great possibilities might lay ahead of me. Letters from different division level colleges began to poor in. Letters as far south as Tennessee to as far north as Rhode Island began to come in, and it felt as though I was about to embark on a new journey in my football career. One of the schools that I was focused on was the University of Pittsburgh. During the eighties, the University of Pittsburgh was a successful program under tutelage of Jackie Sherrill. The defense was dominated by one of the few defensive Heisman trophy candidates in history, Hugh Green. I was so taken by Hugh that weekly in art class I would draw pictures of the words Pitt, Hugh, or 99. He was a magnificent player who later played for the Tampa Bay Buccaneers. Dan Marino, Bill Fralic, and Benji Pryor are some of the names that still stay with me today. One name that stood with me was Tom Flynn. Tom Flynn was a junior safety at the time, going into his senior year, and the rumor was that he wasn't going to lose his job to an underclassman. It was also understood that his backup was pretty good as well and that he would probably take Flynn's position upon his graduation. That was a dilemma for me because for years, since Clive had starting playing basketball for Pitt, I had set my mind on going there as well. I would frequently visit the school in the summer and in the fall when my Clive would go back to play in basketball camps and move his belongings into the dorms. I would walk around campus and sit in classes in the cathedral, meet all the athletes, male and female, and would tell them, "I hope to be here next year." I remember the summer going into my senior year while hanging out on campus, telling this female basketball player that I would be there next year, and she got so excited and couldn't wait for me to arrive. There were others who couldn't wait.

Clive had become a megastar at this time. He led the Big East in scoring, was a Big East All-Star and voted to represent the United States in the Pan American Games. Because of his success, I had access to many things as an eighteen-year old and I couldn't wait to take full advantage of this access. Unfortunately, my ego and short-term perspective blurred my decision-making process that eventually closed the door to my matriculation into Pitt. My success on the field and the distinction of coming from a school such as New Rochelle led me to believe I was entitled to play and play immediately. I didn't want to wait behind Tom Flynn, and I definitely didn't want to wait behind his backup. At that time, I believed positions were a lock, and that any new comer had to wait his turn to see the field. Of course, now I know that when one competes, the best man wins. This was a learning experience for me, because little did I realize at the time that in my journey as a college athlete, I would be placed in situations where I would draw on these moments to step up and show why I deserved to be on the field and be recognized as one of the best at this game called football.

Time was moving along, and I soon had to decide what school I was going to attend in the fall. I visited schools in Massachusetts, Connecticut, and Staten Island. Wagner College was in Staten Island and they were pursuing me heavily. Two years prior they had recruited A Rowe, Daren's older brother, who made that remarkable play on the goal line against Kingston. He now had become a Division III All-American and would possibly have an opportunity to play in the NFL. That was intriguing to me: being able to play side-by-side with A Rowe and also have an opportunity to go further. My next visit was with the University of Connecticut. This was a heartbreaking visit because no visit took place. At this time Daren had received an official visit to the school to play basketball and I was also asked by the head coach to come up and meet him and visit the school. The school wasn't as big as it is today. They played in the Yankee conference against schools like UMass, Northeastern, and other schools that were looking at me. I liked UConn as an option because L.C., who was the quarterback of the state championship team with A Rowe, was the quarterback there and he was a highly-targeted player with possible opportunities in the future. I was brought to the coaches' office to see him and asked to wait outside while he was seeing other recruits. As I watched recruits come and go from the office, I wondered to myself when I would get called in. Whenever the door opened, and a recruit would exit, my heart thumped because I knew I would be next to be called in. I was never called in!

One of the assistant coaches came out and said, "Coach isn't seeing any more recruits today, so thank you for coming." The head coach never came out to meet or greet me personally, so I didn't know what to think or do. I was in total shock and I was angry. I wanted to throw something or kick something, but what I really wanted to do at that point was get the hell out of there. Joe Fosina drove D. Rowe and me to UConn—the same Joe Fosina who was walking down the walkway with Mr. Flowers, Mr. Bailey, and Mr. Holly years earlier. He had always been there for us New Ro athletes. His entire family had always been there for the kids who had come out of New Rochelle Pop Warner Youth Tackle League. Joe brought us there because he was heading to UConn for his job. Joe's company, Rawlings Sporting Goods, cleaned the uniforms for many college teams in the tri-state area, including the New York Yankees. To this day he still cleans the Yankees uniforms. But Joe had brought us up early that morning to do his job. He headed back home and wouldn't return until the next day. L.C., his close teammate, and Vernon Hargraves Sr., the basketball coach, arranged some activities for us. We attended the UConn basketball game that night, featuring Earl Kelly. He was a star from New Haven, Connecticut, who was destined to make it to the NBA. He was also a friend to Clive who he played with on the Big East All-Star team. Hanging out that night softened some of the blow of not being seen by the football coach. I guessed there was no need to see me: the football coach had seen all that he needed to see, and my play wasn't good enough for him to warrant seeing me. Joe came back the next day and picked us up and drove us back. On the way home, I told him what had happened, and although he felt bad for me, he quickly offered an alternative suggestion.

"Why don't you visit Southern, where Mike and Sonny play?"

I said, "Where's that?"

He said, "In New Haven, Connecticut, only an hour from New Rochelle."

Southern had recruited in total seven players from New Rochelle in the past two years. Southern was being coached by Southern Hall of Fame Coach Kevin Gilbride who went on to the NFL to coach hall of fame quarterbacks, Warren Moon and Eli Manning. He had established Southern as a Division II powerhouse, which just came out of a 9-1 season, and the team was made up of mostly sophomores and juniors. That initially didn't sound too promising to me, because it sounded a lot like Pitt and me having to "wait my turn again" and I wasn't up for that. Joe suggested I speak with Sonny Fernandez; he played cornerback at New Ro and had become starting cornerback at Southern Connecticut.

Sonny stood 5 8″, maybe 5 9″, and a solid 185. Although Sonny took football seriously, his demeanor was always one of a calm storm. He played the position like he was born to play it. When it was time for him to "force" from the outside, one would think one was hit by someone 6 2″and 200 pounds. Sonny told me I could play at Southern. He said Coach Gilbride wanted me bad and that he scheduled me to come in and talk to me. I initially didn't want to go to Southern because it wasn't Division I. I believed I was better than that and that I was able to play at a school like Pitt, Syracuse, or any of the "big-time" schools at that time. Southern sent one of its coaches to visit with me at New Ro. His name was Coach Rusty Dunne. Coach Dunne was the wide receiver coach, short in stature, that had also recruited New Rochelle players years before. He laid out Southern's academic offerings and the football schedule for the upcoming year. In regard to school majors, I wanted to major in modeling. When I said that to him he busted out laughing!

"Modeling," he said.

I did a fashion show in high school and I was asked to attend a modeling school by an agent in the crowd that night, and I was seriously interested in seeking a career in modeling or acting. My girlfriend at the time had done some soap opera work and TV shows. She eventually went on to become one of the first daytime, home show hostesses. Well Southern didn't have modeling as a major or minor, but they did have a fine arts department where I ended up majoring in theater. As we sat in one of the Assistant Principal's conference rooms, Coach Dunne talked about the history of Southern football and the challenging upcoming season. What intrigued me about the upcoming schedule was that it consisted of games against Division I-AA teams, such as Rhode Island, and top Division II teams, such as Indiana University of Pennsylvania and Bucknell. The one game I was most interested in was the upcoming game in California against Cal Poly, Saint Louis Obispo. It was a diverse schedule that gave me an opportunity to still play against good competition and hopefully get recognized. At this point in my life, I had not been on a plane since I landed in 1974, and I wanted to go to California. Coach Dunne made it clear that the whole team would not be going, only those that made the traveling squad. I said to myself, "I want to go to California." During this period, I received my official acceptance letter from the University of Pittsburgh, and I was battling with myself on whether I should take a shot at Pitt or attend Southern. Going through my head were the great summer visits with Clive and the many girls I met who were actually chaperoning while Clive was in practice or in meetings. I would miss that experience and those times, but a bigger objective was on hand, and that was to begin playing football right away.

I decided to attend Southern Connecticut State University to further my education and play football. One of the differences between Division I and Division II is that one provides scholarship assistance and the other doesn't. That was a difficult decision, because my mother couldn't afford college; we barely had enough to make ends meet. Southern had put together a generous financial aid package that supported me through my college experience and all I had to do was get loans for yearly extracurricular expenses and books. The next thing was to visit the school. The visit was scheduled for me to attend the spring game, which was in April, and to meet Coach Gilbride. When March rolled around I was excited and ready to go. By this time the latest newspaper awards were being given out to the top football players in Westchester County. On these lists I wasn't ranked very high. I was third-team Westchester County and honorable mention All-County. The players that made first or second team were players on teams that I played well against or teams that didn't play the caliber football we played in Westchester, New York. That really upset me because, once again, I believed that who I was as a football player and person was not being recognized and that I was a forgotten outsider who was an afterthought. I had developed a Rodney Dangerfield complex: "I get no respect." This lack of recognition provided the motivation, incentive, and anger to make everyone notice me and force them to deal with me one way or another.

So, on a sunny afternoon in April 1983, I attended Southern's annual spring game and festivities. Joe Fosina once again drove me up. He scheduled his uniform pickup around my visit to the school. He would leave after he did his business and I would spend the night there and return home Sunday with Sonny. As I look back at this point in my tale, I say to myself, "I must have lost my mind." During high school, the football team was looked at as the next coming of Christ. We couldn't do any wrong and we were like celebrities in the school. The beer incident tarnished us a little, but for me, being able to play in the Iona prep game just gave me a little more Chutzpah around campus. We even smoked on little cigars after a win as we walked home from the school down North Avenue. That over-the-top confidence went with me on my visit to Southern, which almost resulted in a withdrawal of the offer to attend Southern.

On this sunny afternoon at Southern's game, the families of the players playing in the game, as well as recruits' parents, sat along the hillside of the field. Back then, Southern had an old grass field with places bare with no grass at all—just dust. But it was Southern's and it had a long history of having football played on these grounds. Plus, as part of the recruiting sales pitch, we were told that Southern was to have a new turf field by my sophomore year. As I watched the game from high atop the hill, I witnessed how much bigger these college boys were. I was excited but at the same time questioned if I really wanted to go on this journey. You could hear the hits high above the field into the hill; balls were being thrown sixty to seventy yards down the field for touchdowns. There was an amazing tight end by the name of Travis Tucker. He stood 6 3″, 235 pounds, and ran a 4.6 forty-yard dash. The ball just stuck to his hands whenever it touched him. After the first half was over, I walked up the hill to get something to eat from the little concession stand. Upon my return, I remembered that I brought one of the cigars with me, so I lit it up on top of the hill looking down onto the field. Out of nowhere, Sonny came running up the hill and told me to put it out and that one of the coaches saw me with the cigar and that it wouldn't be good if Coach Gilbride saw it in my mouth. If the expression on Sonny's face was any inclination of what kind of Coach Gilbride was, I would be in big trouble if he saw me. What happened was one of the assistants at the time, Coach Richard Cavanaugh, saw me from the sidelines and told Sonny to run and tell me to put it away. Sonny wasn't upset with me but he made it clear that behavior wasn't going to fly at Southern Connecticut State University. When the spring game ended, I went down to the field to meet Coach Dunne and the rest of the players. The players were impressive. Players were from Brooklyn, Queens, upstate New York, New Jersey, and small towns in between like Deep River, Connecticut. There were also some players with some interesting names like "Big Bitch," "Bam Bam," and "The Chink." One impressive player who was from Brooklyn, New York, played outside linebacker and his name was Van Clive Johnson. Van was an imposing figure with a personality that often pushed or crossed the line. His presence had me shaking in my pants and my heart beating twice as fast as it did prior to meeting him, which spurred my subconscious to yearn for that cigar. After I met most of the players, I waited for Sonny in the field house while he took his shower. After that he brought me up to the coaches' office where I met with Coach Dunne and sat and talked about the game. He asked if I enjoyed it and said they would like to see me out there. He told me we were going in to see Coach Gilbride and that he was anxious to meet me and know the status of my decision to attend Southern or not. I hadn't turned eighteen yet and my fragile senses were on ends as I was about to meet with Coach Gilbride. As I entered, he greeted me with a half-smile and wanted to know how I was doing and if I got a chance to see the game. (I took that as a sign he didn't see me with the cigar in my mouth.) I told him I enjoyed myself and looked forward to seeing more of the school. He made it clear that he wanted me there and the schedule would be challenging this year and he was looking for players that would help Southern be successful. I took that to mean he was asking me to make the decision to come to Southern. I believe I told him I made my decision to attend Southern and that I was ready to sign my letter of intent. On the twenty-third day of April, a rainy Sunday morning, I signed my letter of intent to be a student athlete at Southern Connecticut. Later that afternoon, I jumped in the car heading home to New Ro with Sonny Fernandez, Mike West, and Big Bitch.

Chapter Six

The Restart

After returning home, the word got out that I was attending Southern Connecticut State University. People were somewhat baffled that I hadn't chosen the University of Pittsburgh where Clive went; and were surprised that I was heading to a school that most people from New Rochelle never heard of. It was okay with me though. I told them that New Rochelle had a few players who were already attending the school and shared the names they were already familiar with. I appeared to have most people's approval. I say most people because, one must realize, there are always those who one thinks are one's friends but really are not. Some become envious of one's success, even though in one's own eye one may feel one hasn't achieved what one set one's self out to achieve. But for now, I was content and anxious to get started on preparing to get to preseason camp in August.

There were a few hurdles to overcome before August, however. The first was gaining weight. During high school, my weight stood still at a mere 170 pounds at 6 3″. I was tall and lanky. My speed and aggressive play allowed me to "hit them" before "they hit me," which was crucial to my success on the field but moving forward and playing with college players like Big Bitch, Melvin Wells, and Van Clive Johnson, I would definitely need more weight and more speed to be successful. The other hurdle to overcome was to learn a new position. At New Ro, I played stand-up defensive end, a position that allowed me to use my speed to get around the end and attack the quarterback with malice in my heart. It was a position where most of the time I was outweighed by offensive linemen who were often times fifty pounds heavier than me. While the other schools that had been recruiting me saw me as a possible stand up outside linebacker, which mimics the high school defensive end position, most of them saw me playing in one or two years after I gained another twenty, thirty pounds, or more. That appeared to be a mountain that was far off and too high to climb in such a short time, which was one of the reasons I didn't follow through on the other colleges. Coach Gilbride saw something else, however: he pictured me as a defensive back and free safety, playing twelve yards of the ball, using my speed to get off the hash marks, and transferring the rage onto an un-expecting receiver. I had never played defensive back or free safety before. Earl was the free safety and Jim Yacone was our strong safety, so I had an idea of what to do, but to actually know how to line-up, back-pedal, and break on the board, I was a fish out of water.

I knew I had a lot of work to do over the summer—and so did Sonny. Sonny was going into his junior year and he was getting ready to follow-up on the successful season of 9-1 the year before.

Like most graduations, New Ro's was in late July and it was held on the football field behind the school. As I sat there looking around, thoughts ran through my head about many of these faces I would not see in a long time or ever again. As I looked down at my feet planted on the grass on the thirty-five-yard line, it hit me that my days sacking quarterbacks, running down running backs, and even facing the Demateo brothers had come to an end. What would my future become; would I make the traveling team at Southern, or worse, would I even make it into college? I would be the first in my immediate family to attend college and the second in our entire family tree to attend— Clive being the first. There was a lot of uncertainty swirling around in my head. My grades weren't the best; I had barely received a C+ average. It wasn't that I wasn't smart, because in Isaac my grades were good, and I was doing geometry in ninth grade; I had allowed my compulsion to be accepted interfere with my responsibility of being a student first and an athlete second. Even though I was shy—yes, shy—when it came to speaking to girls, I didn't have a hard time getting one, mostly because they came to me. That lack of focus brought on anxiety, frustration, and concern, so I was always on the edge, feeling inadequate. My mother had steady employment working as the "kitchen lady" in the New Rochelle School system as well as a nursing assistant at night. Years of working with the elderly and sick took a toll on her back and legs, and it became harder and harder for her to handle it all. She came home many times frustrated and angry with me for not taking care of the home responsibilities while she was away. I had to pick my brother up from daycare when he was small, and a few times I was late. I had to pick up the government meals of cheese, eggs, cereal, and milk for low-income families and sometimes I forgot. I didn't realize how much my mom depended on me to be a contributor to our household and not only a consumer of it. These adolescent, pre-collegiate years had become pretty difficult, and my relationship with my mother had become strained.

While my responsibilities at home remained paramount, which was basically making sure my brother was safe, I had to find time to get in shape as well as learn the defensive back position. I give all the credit to Sonny Fernandez for making me into the defensive back that I turned out to be. For the next two years, I had Sonny available as a mentor to show me the way. The first thing was to get my weight up. Sonny scheduled time to meet at Iona, the local college, to start my weightlifting training. I rarely lifted in high school. Like I said before, I relied on my talent of speed, anger, and determination to make plays. Sonny knew that would not be enough to play at the next level, and so my training began under his supervision. Sonny also taught me day-in and day-out the position of DB: the stance, weaving technique, and coming out of the breaks. He spent many hours demonstrating to me and teaching me not only the mechanics of the position but also the mindset of the DB. The free safety, he said, was like the quarterback of the defense. I would have to learn the defense's coverage and make adjustments when necessary. I would later learn first hand that my mental capacity would need to be raised if I were to be successful. I thank Sonny Fernandez to this day for his time and patience with me. For without him, and his care for my success, I don't believe my college career would have been as successful as it turned out to be.

While my football life was moving forward, it wasn't as pleasant and rewarding for many of my teammates who were the "stars" of the team—the ones who had taught me and demonstrated how to play the game of football and what it took to be a champion. Out of the many great players on the team, only a few of us had the opportunity to go on and play at the college level. Hubert Parris went on to New York Tech; Jim Yacone went on to West Point; "T-Fudge" went on to Hofstra; and Rob Castagna went on to Central Connecticut. The rest of the guys didn't get recruited and I wasn't sure why. The backbone of our defense wasn't me. It was Earl, Icky, and Todd Depaso, with a very good supporting cast. Those guys were our vibrant, spirited leaders that set the standard of play for many of us. When I would lose it on the field, Earl would pull me back and say, "Don't get kicked out of the game. Get them back on the next play." I felt sorry for those guys because many of them came from the same tough, blue-collar-working families like I did that could have used the opportunity to have their sons go off and play college football on a scholarship or financial aid. The other four guys and myself were blessed to have the opportunity to play football on the next level; and because of this opportunity, it paved the way for a better life for me then, my future, and my future family.

The summer had come to a close and it would soon be time to head off to college. I was venturing on a new journey, a journey of independence, the unfamiliar and the unknown. I had prepared myself the best I could for the unknown. I had gained ten pounds; I was now 185 pounds of more muscle and in good running shape. I had stopped by Al's Barber Shop a week before to get a haircut, so I felt good, looked good, and was ready to go. I remember riding up to school with my mom, my stepdad, and my brother. My dad had a sense of humor that I wasn't always sure how to take.

He would say things like, "Are you sure you're going to college? College is a serious place."

I would say, "Yes."

He would reply, "Oh sure." Even when we got to the school and I moved in some of my things, he would say, "Are you sure they'll allow you to stay here?"

"Of course," I replied.

"Oh sure." I knew he was joking; he would joke all the time to get me animated. But then he would start laughing. I guess he got a kick out of getting me bothered. I miss him and his humor very much, and I believe my mom and my little brother do too. He and mom divorced just after three years of marriage, but he remained around, mainly because at the time my brother and I were still young; I was into sports and mom had to work multiple jobs to keep the lights on and a roof over our heads. One might ask, *Didn't she have help from my stepdad?* Yes and no. He was a master chef who worked in the finest restaurants and country clubs in Westchester, New York. After work, he would bring home meals he made that day that were nothing I had ever encountered before. Up until then, my experiences with exotic foods were strictly Jamaican, and experiencing those master chef creations was something else. To say the least, we never went hungry and we ate well. The problem wasn't that he didn't care about mom or us; it was the fact he was dealing with the disease of alcoholism. It had affected his relationship with mom and his job. There were nights growing up when I would hear them verbally fighting in the room after he would come home late from work, so intoxicated that he couldn't walk up the stairs. There were other nights when he would climb up the fire escape to get in our second-floor apartment, waking up the families that lived downstairs. One night, the fight was so bad that it woke me out of bed because I heard my mother screaming. I had had enough, and I was going to confront my stepdad. When I opened the door to their bedroom, I saw a puddle of blood in the center of the bed. I was now scared and looked at my dad and told him to leave us alone and pushed him out the door. His eyes were bloodshot-red from drinking and blood was dripping from his hands. He looked at me and told me to move, but I didn't; he stood there for a moment, grunted for a minute, then left. Mom comforted me and said she was okay and I should go back to bed now. As I lay there, I was overtaken by mixed feelings of anger and helplessness. I couldn't protect my mom, and dad had driven his relationship with her down the drain. I believe that those experiences from living with Aunt Louise, and then the adolescent years of violence in the home, left me angry and wanting. Wanting *love, peace, and happiness.*

So, as we all stood there on the front steps of the football dorm and I prepared to head over to the field house to report into camp, my mom looked at me as she always did and said, "It's going to be okay. Work hard. You sure you can do it?"

I said, "Yes, mom."

She gave me twenty dollars and said, "This is all I have; make it last."

I turned to my brother and gave him a big hug, high-five, and kiss and told him to come to some of my games with mom. He said, "Okay."

Then I turned to my dad. He was not a man of many words, but when he did speak in his baritone voice, it was often a joke questioning my ability or commitment. He then said to me, "Do well," with a smile and returned to the car. Those few words carried a lot of weight. The way he said the words were like code for, *I'm proud of you.* And that was my plan: to make him, mom, and New Ro proud of me.

I made my way over to the field house where all the players were meeting and receiving their instructions for the day and room assignments. I don't recall who my roommate was at this time, but I do remember the personalities that came alive once I entered the gym. There was "Bam Bam," Arbuckle, "The Chink," Big Melvin, Big Bitch, Van Clive Johnson, Kerry Taylor, Jeff Stoutland, Mike West, and, of course, Sonny—a familiar face. I was nervous as heck. That superstar, "Hollywood," cigar-smoking kid was with the big boys now, and I realized that many of those players were stars in their high schools, and also, too, had played Division I football. But something brought us all together at this time and in this place to experience the game of football together. As we all stood around, Coach Campbell—the offensive line coach, a big man—barked out the instructions of where to get our room keys and roommates. After that, we were to return to the field house for a team meeting and receive the camp schedule. Even though many players welcomed me, I still felt like an outsider again. I was welcomed mostly because I was from New Ro, and New Ro football had established itself at Southern with Mike West and Sonny. I was the next New Ro guy who was to fill in and let them know what goes on down in Westchester. Checking into the room was the first time I ever saw a college dorm room. On my previous visit with Sonny, I stayed in an off-campus apartment, which is where most upperclassmen lived. As I put my bags down, sat on the bed and looked around, once again I realized that my college career had begun and that I couldn't go home and face mom, dad, my brother, or New Ro without being successful. But I was scared as I headed over to the gym for the first meeting. As I headed through the front glass door of Moore Field House, I could hear harmonized singing coming from the area I was heading towards. As I made my way, I came across a circle of players in the middle of the gym; they were the ones singing. They were singing a Temptations song, "Just my Imagination." Not to be stereotypical, but most of the players were African American. I say that because it was frequently the same group singing the old Motown song, as you will see later on, but not always. At times, the leader of the "Owls Singers" would try to encourage the white players to join in and add a little doo-wop or base sound when needed, which always brought out a big roar from the team. Bam Bam would frequently add a tune and Arbuckle too. The atmosphere was lively, full of energy and excitement. Southern had come off a 9-1 season the year before and was looking to have a big season this coming fall. Moments later, the gym got quiet as the players started to settle down when Coach Gilbride walked in. Coach stood about 6 3″ tall at 200 to 215 pounds, which allowed him to size up and look most players in the eye—which could be more intimidating than expected— and he had a deep voice that filled the room with clear and precise articulation. I thought that he carried a heavy stick and the guys would be scared of him, but that wasn't the case. The players respected him because of his commitment to winning, to the team, and commitment to bringing out the best in each and every player on the team. I would soon learn how much he loved winning and what it would take to join the ranks of a college football player and go to Cali.

My initial impression was wrong, not by much, but enough to say *I'll stick around and endure the journey*. I thought that there wouldn't be any laughing or playing around. Quite the contrary, there were a lot of jokes being made of other players as Coach brought up instances that accrued years past. Kerry Taylor was always the loudest during this time. He always had a funny remark to make—funny enough to even get a smile out of Coach sometimes. Kerry was from Gorton High School, the school that beat New Ro in the playoff game in high school. He always was in the middle of everything: singing, telling jokes, and making touchdowns. I eventually learned a lot from Kerry and the upperclassmen, that even though he was loud off the field, he was always business on the field.

In the eighties, there were not as many safeguards around practices. The first day of practice consisted of three, where as today, there are a limited and maximum amount of practices allowed. I remember the days being hot and humid and dust flying up after every tackle due to the lack of grass in certain areas of the field. Coming from New Rochelle, a city of moderate wealth, we had the resources from tax dollars to support a challenging curriculum in school, as well as to have quality facilities to play in. Southern, at the time, was on the brink of breaking through the threshold of moving its athletic programs to the next level, and winning would be the catalyst to make that happen. One of the selling points of me coming to Southern was that by sophomore year Southern would have a new artificial turf football stadium on campus. I believed I had made the right choice in going to Southern because I would be part of building something big for the future. However, until then, practice was held in the back of the Moore Field House on a hundred-yard dusty field. Playing on that field, I got another sense of what football was really about. It actually taught me to reevaluate how I played the game. The game isn't about being a showboat and letting everyone know how great you are. It's not about playing in great facilities, or even playing with the best players. Having less-lifted the shades from my eyes to see that to be the best and be successful depended on what I, as an individual, could bring to the table with. The constant reminder of this occurred from the sidelines while I was watching the upper class run plays with the dust flying up from underneath the feet of the running backs as they cut and swerved their way through the hole, only to be met by the middle linebacker with a crashing blow.

When the dust cleared, Coach Gilbride would say, "Do it again."

I would stand with the other freshman and learned from what I was seeing until my name was called. After the first two days or so, I realized that football was a serious thing, even at this level, and for me to make it through the week, through the year, my mental approach to the game would have to be adjusted.

The next question was, *How do I get noticed?* Those that know football know that the nonstarters or underclassmen are responsible for running plays for the starters, or in Southern's case, "the blue team." Most times, freshman and sophomores run the plays as a training ground to prepare the upperclassmen and starters for the first game of the season. The first time they called on the freshmen, I was hoping I wouldn't get called out, but as I stood there, Sonny—from the other side of the ball—called out my name and told me to get in there and run a play. Yes, I was hesitant, but my ego popped up again and said, "Can't have no one call you out and you not respond"; so, I took up the challenge and jumped in the huddle with the other freshman to run the plays. I had played running back in the Pop Warner days, so I decided to jump in the running back position, a position that no one liked to take on because it meant you would probably get hit every play by the starting defensive front line that consisted of the names I mentioned earlier. I knew, however, that if I wanted to get on the field and play I had to be seen. If I wanted to make the trip to California, I had to play like I had never played before. There were another thirty freshman that came in and had the same aspirations as I did. Unfortunately, only ten would make the trip, and I wanted to be one of the ten. So, as I ran scout team, I had two objectives: one, not to get hit; and two, to make the starters look bad. If I made them look bad, the coaches would remember my name and notice the freshman that was giving a "good look." I worked hard on scout team and doing so didn't go unnoticed. A few times our middle linebacker, Jeff Stoutland, the leader of the defense, smart, intense, and handsome—a Long Island tough guy—got upset with me. I frustrated him because I made a lot of long runs through the defense and I made it difficult for them and the rest of the defense to get clean shots on me, which was my first objective. Coach Dunne, the coach that recruited me, ran the offensive plays for the freshman and he would always encourage me to continue to do well. He often smiled after a big gain, because he knew if the freshman were doing well by effort and outcomes, it would be good for Coach Gilbride's evaluations, as well as himself.

After running scout team, the freshman got a chance to show what they had learned from the assistant coaches' meeting and whether or not they were picking things up by paying attention to the upperclassmen. The night before practices, the position assistant coaches would meet with their players and implement new defenses and each player's additional responsibilities. What we learned the first night was about to be showcased in front of Coach Gilbride. I was given first shot at safety in cover-three zone coverage. Coverage three is a basic defensive back coverage that aligns the safety in the middle of the field; his responsibility is to cover the middle-third of the field and not allow any receiver get past him. To me, however, it felt like I was responsible for everything that was thrown in the air in the other two-thirds of the field, including my middle-third. But when you've never played the position before, it can be intimidating and overwhelming just trying to do the right thing and be in the right place and not make any mistakes. Well, the first day I wasn't in the right place, but I was doing the right thing—the right thing in that wherever the ball went, I went. I hustled to the ball, made big hits, and maintained a high level of energy. The wrong thing was that I should not have been making plays at the line of scrimmage or knocking down passes on the other side of the field. The safety has to be disciplined and stay in his area until the ball is thrown. I was just running all over the place trying to make plays everywhere. The first day was not a good day and I would hear more about that at the position meeting later that night.

Steve Bush was the defensive back coach. He played at Southern a few years earlier and was also the schools all-time interception leader with eighteen. He was a personable coach that I felt I could go to and ask questions, and he would take the time to explain the answer. In this first meeting, I got the first chance to meet and socialize with the other upper-class defensive backs and other freshman. As we sat there waiting for Coach to come into the locker room to go over the day, a lot of chatter and jokes were being made about the day and that if you wanted to play, you better be a quick learner. The other freshman and I sat there quietly as we listened to the indirect advice being provided. When Coach came in, the first thing he did was have everyone reintroduce himself.

When it got to me, I said, "Pat Morrison, New Rochelle High." Sonny immediately let everyone know that there was another New Ro Player on the team and that they needed to watch out. Coach smiled and chuckled as other players from competing high schools looked on in disgust. One particular player that didn't appear to fit in with the rest of the group sat against the wall smiling and taking it all in. He stood about 6 1″, 160 pounds, had long blond hair, wore baggy shorts (before they were common), beach flip-flops, and had a laid-back smile to match. He introduced himself as Rick Atkinson from Deep River. We all looked at each other and said, "Where's Deep River?" He looked more like a surfer from California, and from then on he was called "California Boy." He said Deep River was towards the shore, off Route 9. None of us from urban New York areas knew where that was, so we all just laughed it off. As Coach Bush reviewed the first day's practice, I realized that I needed to understand the position more if I wanted to play; and to understand how to play college football, I would have to study the three-and-a-half-inch playbook that was handed out.

The next couple of days were rough. Trying to keep up with the implementation of new coverage and making the right adjustments became a challenge for me. The safety is like the quarterback of the defense, so if I didn't make the right adjustment (audible), the defensive backfield would be out of position to cover the possible play the offense was about to make. Over the next week, freshmen started to leave the team. It was either because they didn't expect to be challenged at this level or just couldn't compete at this level. Although Southern was a Division II team, Coach Gilbride ran a first-class program that ran like it was a Division I program. By the second week, the freshman class was coming together as a unit. Initially, I was battling with some players from Westchester County high school conferences, but by the middle of the week, I had solidified the position as my own. One of the things that set me apart from the other safeties that were brought in was my hitting and tackling ability; that made up for my challenges in getting the defense lined up in the right coverage. When I would tackle a player, once again it was with a sense of intention, hostility, malice, and anger that just presented itself on the field, and it would take a lot to come down from that high. That sense of heightened intensity solidified my position with the coaches that I had to be on the field somehow. As I was dismantling freshman and upper-class receivers,

California Boy was quietly making a name for himself too. He had a canny ability to be in the right place the majority of the time to intercept the ball. His ability to make ankle tackles and intercept the ball was incredible, and he too solidified himself as the starting right corner. By the time the second week of camp was over, we all had become new men. Physically, many of us—although we had lost weight from the constant exercise, running and hitting in the August sun—were in tremendous shape. My ability to run one hundred yards was effortless and my ability to get off the hash and make plays became second nature. But that was just the first phase of my plan to play college football: to make the team. The second phase was to make the traveling team so I could make the trip to sunny California. The starting defensive backfield at this time was Sonny, Chucky from Hamden Connecticut, Wade Baldwin from New Jersey, and Carl-something. Because of my development, Coach Gilbride had Wade, who was a transfer safety from Arizona State, learn strong safety as well as backup to Chucky who was a senior. I was told that Coach was looking to have me play at safety as soon as I got the coverages adjustments down. I was still having trouble making the right audible when the ball was on the hash and when the offense came out in a specific formation. Coach wouldn't feel confident in me until I got it down one hundred percent. Rick, on the other hand, was playing great and immediately moved into the backup position behind the senior, Carl. It would be just a matter of time before he would be on the field and making a name for himself.

Camp was over right before Labor Day weekend. We all would be heading home to see our families and get some good home-cooked food and loving. But first, the list was put up on the wall in the locker room. There was a line of freshman, sophomores, and senior players who stood there searching for their names. There were some juniors, as well as sophomores, who would not make the trip, and it was understood that only twenty-four players would make the trip. As I made my way to the wall and looked at the white sheet of paper with the typed-out names of the players, my eyes strolled down to see if I was one of the twenty-four. I saw my name, "Pat Morrison, freshman defensive back." I was so happy; a big smile came across my face as Sonny stood there to congratulate me. As I looked at him, it felt like he knew all along that I was going, but he couldn't say anything. There were five freshmen that were chosen: me, Rick Atkinson, Marty Durkin, who played strong safety, Scott Meursereau, defensive tackle, and one offensive player. It was a privilege to be chosen because it showed that Coach recognized my ability and was committed to giving me and the selected other four a chance to compete and play. Our test would come during the junior varisty games. There were JV games scheduled for freshman to hone their skills, knowledge, and confidence. I remember our starting defensive secondary, with Marty at strong safety, me at safety, and Ricky anchoring the sidelines, was like pure terror for the opposing JV teams we played. I thought I was crazy and insane playing with Icky and Earl back in high school, but Marty Durkin would have fit right in with the New Ro Crew with his antics on the field. Marty was from Bynum Hills High School, another Westchester school in another division. Marty could run and hit. He would hit you with intention and with no regard for his own safety. I could see what was forming around me, a set of top recruits that would lead Southern into the future under the tutelage of Coach Gilbride. Being selected to the traveling team also meant we were also on the varsity team throughout the year, which meant we also had the opportunity to play and be in competition for a spot on the varsity team. As the season went along, changes started to happen. Chuck Goodwin, who was a senior, was having back issues and forced to come out a few games. He would be replaced by Wade Baldwin, who then was replaced at safety by a junior, Glenn Ricky. I was better than Glenn and I thought I should have been in there, but that wasn't the case. Coach Bush would tell me that Coach wasn't confident in me yet getting the coverage down, so he wasn't ready to put me in. Marty was the third-team safety behind Wade and me, but because of his tenacity on the field he was later moved to backup Chucky, which eventually lead to Marty starting midway through the season. So Marty was the first of the "Super Freshman" to play on the varsity team. They started to call us the Super Freshman because we were definitely turning heads. I was happy for him and although I played on special teams, it wasn't the same as being out there all the time; and it also showed me again that if I could play up to my potential and get the coverage down, my time would come as well. Coach scheduled a lot of difficult teams and the next one up was the University of Rhode Island, a Division I-AA team. Division I-AA meant these players would be on scholarship and most likely would be bigger, stronger, and faster than us. We had big and fast players too, but not as big as them. What made Southern players different was that many of the players had the talent and the heart to play the game, but unfortunately our "measurables" didn't always fit the traditional, expected numbers to play at a Division I level. Some players may have been too undersized to play D-I, too short as a linebacker or lineman, or too light like Rick, Mearsereu, and me; but ability to play and coaching made us able to compete with anyone. The game against Rhode Island was a good one; we battled back and forth throughout the game and could have beaten them. During the game, the starting corner was Carl, and he got burnt two times for touchdowns. Coach Gilbride had had enough and decided to put Rick in. We all looked around for Rick, but he was ready to go and was already on the field. One thing Coach expected was for everyone to pay attention to the game—even if someone was a third-string player and the possibility of him playing was slim. A player never knew when his number might be called, but when it was, he better be aware of what was going on in the game and ready to play. Well, Rick was ready to play. Within minutes, the first pass made to his side of the field...he intercepted it! Then, after a turnover by the offense and Rhode Island moving down the field again, he intercepted another one. It was amazing and exciting to watch California Boy do his thing. The score was close, but we ended up losing the game by a touchdown and Rick ended up with three interceptions for the game. That performance by Rick sealed his position for the next four years at Southern. I, on the other hand, didn't see much playing time. Once again, I played special teams, which was mostly running down on kickoffs and punt return coverages. That was okay, though, because I did not yet feel comfortable making the defensive calls and, quite honestly, I was still a bit apprehensive about playing with the big boys and getting hit every play. I felt it would take some more time to be comfortable enough to be out there, and by default, it did. I would, however, have to start feeling comfortable or I would not get out of New Haven, Connecticut, and would get left behind when the trip to California came around. Our record up to this point in October was 6-1; the only loss was to the University of

Rhode Island. We were getting ready to leave for Cali and I was still on the twenty-four-man roster to go. It was a major game advertised out West as, "The East Meets West." Cal Poly, Saint Luis Obispo at the time was ranked number three in the country in Division II, and I believe Southern may have been seventh. It was an exciting time for me, because other than flying to America in 1974, I had never again been on a plane. So, going to California was going to be an experience I would never forget. We did the touristy things like Disneyland, which for me was living the American experience. Actually, seeing Mickey and Minnie Mouse "live and in person" was something I imagined as a child in England. The guys were loose and taking in all the great sights of the trip as well. Many of the guys from New York had not gone to many places out of the state as well; so not seeing more of America wasn't an English thing, it was an economic thing. We were there for three days. We flew in the first day and settled into our hotel rooms. The second day we had practice at one of the Cal Poly fields. Cal Poly was a far cry from Southern Connecticut University. Their facilities made ours look like an elementary school waiting for funding. It was beautiful and plush, and we took every moment we could to take it all in; and realized we didn't come this way to take in sun alone, but to win the game which would bring a perfect ending to a great trip away from home. The day of the game was sunny, eighty-eight degrees with blue skies, and the stands were full, with about twenty thousand spectators. It was like we were playing in the Super Bowl. There were signs that read "East vs. West" stretched all around the stadium walls and throughout the stands. Those signs just got us more hyped up and ready to play more than ever. Van Clive Johnson was always ready. He was from Boys High in Brooklyn, New York, and he took the game as a challenge between New York and California, which from his perspective and all of ours, there was no comparison. New York consists of rough, struggling blue-collar families making ends meet with very little. Our perception of California was that it was all sunshine, blue pacific waters, palm trees, tranquility, and amazing facilities; life was good in California, which translated to soft. We were not going to let a soft California team beat us—not that day. And, yes, we made fun of Ricky. We told him we expected a big game from him, because he was home with "his people."

He thought it was funny too, and knew we were all in this together. On this sunny California, October day, Southern Connecticut University took on Cal Poly, St. Louis Obispo, which was advertised as the East Meets West showdown. I was on the kickoff team with Marty. Two of the Super Freshman were already in the game and watched closely by Coach Gilbride as to whether we were ready to play or would succumb to the excitement and intensity of the day. We were ready to play our part and Marty would later demonstrate that with a crucial play. Scott Mersereau had also made himself available to play quite a bit at strong outside linebacker. He was on kickoff and special teams as well and ready to make an impactful statement that day and through the next four years.

It's been over thirty years since that game, so I don't recall every moment or every play of the day. However, I do remember the climate, the excitement, and the outcome. I recall I watched most of the game from the sidelines and would head in on the punt coverage, kickoff, and returns. There weren't too many touchdowns scored, mainly because both defenses came ready to play. Southern—of course—we had our own motivations from being underestimated to compete with the number three-ranked team in the nation to refusing to lose after taking a five-hour trip out west. I suppose Cal's motivation was to not lose their ranking to a small, East Coast team that was ranked below them.

Whatever their motivation was, it didn't matter to us; we came to play and win. I recall as it drew towards the end of the game, we had taken a three-point lead by adding a field goal to our score. After the kickoff, Cal Poly was on the move down the field with a third-and-short for the first down and moved onto our side of the fifty-yard line. We couldn't allow that to happen, because then would we be giving them an opportunity to keep the clock going and continue to drive down the field to either kick a field goal to tie, or worse yet, score a touchdown. As I watched intensely from the sideline, I could only admire the demeanor and determination of the guys out on the field. Big Melvin and Van Clive were always animated and keeping the guys up. Jeff Stoutland, the "General," was lining the guys up and holding down the middle with "Sixsmith." These are names and characters I will never forget because they provided an example of how to play the game, which was the best lesson I could have obtained outside of the small locker room three-thousand miles away.

It wasn't any of those upper-class names that would be the hero of the day though. On third-and-short, Marty "Super Freshman Durken" came up from dropping back into coverage and made a third down-and-short stop by tackling the runner short of the first down. Marty's stop was the biggest play of the game. At this point in the game there was less than a minute remaining and Cal Poly had to go for the first down, down the field, or take a shot into the end zone. What would they do, and how would we defend? Because of Cal's do-or-die position this late in the game, Coach Gilbride had a plan, and that plan was to add an additional defensive back to the secondary. This would be our nickel defense, which included me. He looked at me and told me to go in as the nickel back. I was scared as hell, but I ran out there as fast as I could in case he wanted to change his mind. I was scared and smiling at the same time. I got the opportunity to play on and with the starting defense. All three "Super Freshman" were in the game at the same time at a crucial point.

Sonny looked at me and said, "New Ro in the house." I gave the play to Stoutland and I made sure not to mess that up. The worst thing is to not communicate the play to the rest of the players the way it was given to you. After Stoutland gave the defensive front for the linemen, Wade (the starting safety) gave the defensive backfield call, "Nickel Two." Nickel Two meant two deep zones with both safeties on the hash marks. Before leaving the huddle, Sonny reminded me to stay deep and not to let anyone get behind me. There was one thing for sure given this opportunity, it wasn't going to be lost by me getting beat for a long pass. I was going to get as deep as I could, even if I had to run into the stadium parking lot.

On the snap of the ball, I remember putting everything I had learned from camp and the JV games into those few seconds after the ball was snapped. I made sure I took my read steps, made sure I was low, made sure I kept my head on my reads, and, of course, I made sure I got back in my back-pedal and that no one got behind me. I put every hour I had learned up to this point into the closing seconds of the game. As the center snapped the ball to the quarterback and the play was in motion, in my mind everything went silent as the play unfolded in front of me. Cal Poly's All-American tight end had a few catches throughout the game already and I knew they would attempt to get him the ball. He was lined up on the opposite side of where I was lined up, but I kept my eye on him too. I had two receivers to my side, so I had to pay close attention to them as well. As the play unfolded, both receivers to my side began to come towards me, which threatened my side of the field. I had to stay deep and be ready to break on the ball to stop the first down or, even worse, split the safeties up the middle for a touchdown. As they both came towards me, one receiver went across the field to the same side as the tight end, and the other receiver to my side did a short pattern and stopped in front of me. This meant I wouldn't have anyone threatening my area or threatening to get behind me; but I remembered what Sonny said: "stay deep." I did stay deep and didn't jump the short pattern or chase after the other receiver across the field like I did in the early days of camp; and I'm glad I did because as soon as the crossing receiver headed to the opposite hash, the big All-American tight end was heading straight towards my side of the field! I stayed deep and kept my eye on him. The quarterback was under pressure by Big Bitch and from the big boys up front and was under pressure to throw the ball! He reached his arm back in my direction towards the tight end and let it go! The ball and the tight end were heading straight towards my direction, and I realized I was about to be in the middle of probably the most important play of the day. As the ball headed my way, I noticed it was on a low trajectory, and at the same time the quarterback was being hit. The hit caused the ball to lose velocity and fell way short and way out in front of its intended target. I broke on the ball in an attempt to possibly make a play on the ball, as it landed a few feet in front of me and bounced into my hands. The defense held up and met the challenge, and I was so pleased to be part of the moment, even if it was just for a few seconds in time. The offense went back out onto the field and took a knee as the remaining seconds ticked off the clock. Southern won and the East beat the West that afternoon.

Those few seconds on that hot summer afternoon in California everything came full circle from hours and years of commitment, hard work, and staying out of trouble. The opportunity to experience life outside of New Rochelle,

New York, and experience different communities is something I will always be grateful for because I know many of my friends who I played with, who were better than me, never had that opportunity and for that reason, I played for them and New Ro.

Upon our return to campus, we were welcomed and celebrated by our schoolmates with open arms. The school was on a high and local papers wrote articles about Southern's conquest of the West. Coach Gilbride was happy about the victory, but one would never know it by his demeanor. He wasn't a man that would show much elation or emotion over our achievements. There were things he expected his players to accomplish, and doing them wasn't a time to praise, it was more of a time to acknowledge that a player had completed what was expected of him. Of course, I was excited as well as proud to be among those chosen from the JV team to go on the trip, as well as to have something to say about being in the game. Playing in the game lifted my spirits and confidence that I could play on this level and Coach Gilbride thought the same, even if he didn't verbally say it. The fact I was there spoke volumes. As the season progressed, I gained more confidence playing on the JV team, sharpening my skills and knowledge of the position. On JV, which was coached by Coach Dunne, the defensive calls were not so extensive that I had too many checks out of coverage. This allowed me to master the coverages at a slower pace and feel confident out on the field. By the end of the JV season, I had all the coverages down and was ready for the "big time" going into my sophomore year. Throughout my freshman year, I continued to watch and learn from the upperclassmen. They were a great inspiration to me on how to be great football players and teammates. We ended up with an 8-3 record, which was a good record, but we fell short of making a playoff run by one loss.

Sophomore year would turn out to be a very interesting year and the turning point of my collegiate career. Before that would happen, I had to take care of a few academic requirements. The adjustment for me, like other athletes, was a big one. School parties, girls, parties, hanging out—and more girls—got in the way of my studies. As mentioned before, I wasn't an A student, but I wasn't a C student either. I only did enough to get by and that attitude towards education would not fly in college. Thus, the result of my partying and hanging out and girls was a 1.7 GPA. To be eligible to compete in a varsity sport, an athlete needed the minimum 2.0 GPA. I had some work to do and that required I stay for the first half of the summer and take a four-week class to get my grades up and be eligible to play the next year. It was strongly suggested by my position coach, Steve Bush, that I enroll in the Sports Psychology class; which I did. He didn't tell me, however, that Coach Gilbride taught the class. That revelation solidified the fact that I would be in class everyday and ask questions in hopes of being on the good side of Coach. I did what I had to do and received an A- grade on the paper I handed in, which brought my GPA to a 2.3. I was eligible to play in the upcoming fall season and able to officially begin my summer vacation. That summer back home was quite interesting. When I returned home, all the talk was about how well New Ro football players were doing in college and the big hoopla about Big Ben Jefferson. By this time, Big Ben was a senior at New Ro and highly recruited by the major football schools such as USC, Michigan, Nebraska, and the University of Maryland. There was also a lot of talk about Alfredo Rowe (the standout linebacker my sophomore year) out at Wagner University on Staten Island, New York, where he was All-American. I, too, was in the conversation in New Ro, that my play on the field was being noticed and that "I was the man at Southern." Well I wasn't "the man" yet, but the fact that my play on the Southern JV squad and my activities in practice got me noticed in New Haven and in New Rochelle meant that someone was watching and taking notes. Once I was back home, and free from hard practices and social life, it was time to spend some time with my little brother, mom, dad, and my friends who were still around. After graduation from high school, I wasn't sure what happened to many of my friends. Icky went out to California; I lost contact with Earl; and Matt ended up at Virginia State University. He wasn't playing football there—just having fun. He mentioned later to me that from a football perspective, he could compete at Virginia State, but felt there was bias against players from the North. Southerners looked at northerners as basketball players first and football players second. Matt, unfortunately, didn't play at Virginia State, which didn't go unnoticed by other schools.

The summer of my sophomore year felt like any old school summer with nothing to do but sleep in, listen to WBLS radio station, and eat. It was really relaxing, and I spent the rest of my time at Iona College lifting weights or playing basketball with my cousin. That year my cousin was drafted by the Indiana Pacers to play in the NBA but opted to go overseas and play for our home country, England, where he would be guaranteed good money and longevity in the Premier league. I would play against him daily to help him improve on his dribbling skills and in return I would be getting cardiac conditioning. I would also lift weights with Sonny, Mike, and now some of the guys from Mt. Vernon High who also went off to play college football. One of the players, Vinny Brunson, who then was attending the University of Maryland and playing defensive end, told me the word had gotten down to him that I was doing well at Southern and that I should consider transferring. I thought about it and promised I would come down and visit. The summer was lazy and relaxing. I remember going to Sherwood Park beach with mom and my brother. It was an annual trip we would usually go on with family. The summer was closely coming to an end and I was excited because I had an opportunity to be the starting safety my sophomore year. Wade Baldwin was moved to strong safety after Chucky Goodwin's graduation, which left the position open to be won by either the senior, Glenn Ricky, or me. Glenn was not a better athlete than me, but because he knew the defenses it made it natural and respectably his position to lose. So, I had in my mind that I had to win the position. Rick was already starting; Marty was already playing; and it was now my turn to solidify my position on the field. I worked hard for the rest of the summer with my cousin, lifted weights with the guys, and I felt ready to enter preseason camp with the aim of winning the starting the position.

Summer was over, and I was prepared to head back to camp. I had no ride that year because mom had to work, and she couldn't take any days off. I was able to get a ride from one of my friends, Raymond Goodlett, the comedian of the neighborhood. I spent nights with Raymond on his trips to NYC as he delivered mail from the banks in New Rochelle to Lower Manhattan Banks. We would leave at eleven o'clock at night and return around one-thirty in the morning. We often stopped at Sylvia's Restaurant in Harlem for a late-night bite before we would head back to Westchester. Raymond was, and is, one of my best friends who always did for his friends and always provided a good laugh in the process. Raymond drove me back to school with his girlfriend Rene at the time and I made my way over to the dorm where I would be staying, then over to the field house to report in to my second year of Southern football.

Chapter Seven

Changing of the Guard

While it was a wonderful summer being home and seeing my high school schoolmates, it was time to resume my studies and reach the next level of competition in football—and that was to work my way into the starting position. Jeff Stoutland, who was our leader on defense a year before, joined the coaching staff as a graduate assistant for the linebacker group. Coach Bush, the defensive back coach, went on to other college coaching opportunities and was replaced by Coach Dodge, who had played defensive back at Southern a few years earlier. The newcomer to the defense was Jeff Smith, another New Rochelle High player who was a devastatingly-hitting strong safety. Another change I saw was the difference the summer had made in the physical physiques of some of the players. Scott Mearsereau had put on an additional twenty-five pounds; he went from two hundred and fifteen pounds to two hundred and forty pounds, from a stand-up linebacker to a hand-down defensive tackle. In addition to Jeff Smith, we added the next coming at linebacker; we called him "Conan," after the mythical, muscular warrior character seen and read on television and read in comic books. With the many new faces to the team, and the talent pool growing, it was with great disappointment when we heard Marty would not be returning to the team. After the spring game of our freshman year, Marty was told he would be the starting strong safety coming into his sophomore year. Unfortunately, at the same time, and some time during the season, he had developed an injury that continually got worse over the summer and ended up costing him his football career. We were all devastated by the loss of Marty. He brought wit, passion, and humor to the team, which was right in-line with the personality of Southern football. It was also disheartening and a wake-up call, that at any moment an injury could happen, and my own career could end, as soon as it had begun. At the time, I felt that one-third of me had died. Marty was one of the Super Freshmen that Southern was depending on to carry on the torch and now he wasn't there and much of the load was left on Ricky and me. I was more determined than ever to win the starting position this season, by any means necessary. I knew Coach Gilbride wasn't going to give me anything, and that if I wanted to play more, I would have to earn it, even if I was the better athlete.

Coming into camp, the one barrier to me reaching my goal was a senior by the name of Glenn Ricky. Glenn was a good player who had been with Southern since his freshman year. He waited for his turn to come and had rightfully earned the opportunity to be the starting safety his senior year. Unfortunately for him, I had another plan that didn't match up with his. The advantage he had over me was, by this time, I had become very familiar and comfortable with defensive play calls, and I even held my own during the spring game, and made the right calls, but the advantage he had over me was that I had yet to be tested in real competition, in a real game. As such, Coach Gilbride was not yet convinced that I was his guy. I continued to work hard during camp and made my presence known on the field every time I had a chance. Not starting gave me a good platform to demonstrate that I could play with the big boys. Second team players, that were the "red" team, would practice against the first team offense. If I was going to demonstrate that I could make an impact against the first team, well then, that would show I was able to compete against other teams in real competition in a real game. Red team players would also run "scout team" against first team defense. This was another opportunity to show that I could receive as well as deliver the punishment from both sides of the ball. On offense, I would either play running back or wide receiver. I purposely volunteered to play these positions because they were the positions that would get the ball the most and those players would get the most recognition as giving "a good look" for the defense. Giving "a good look" gave a player brownie points with the coach, and I needed to get as many brownie points as I could, so I could be part of that starting defense. I also had confidence in my ability. I often tried to go all out and make the defense look bad. If I made them look bad, two things would happen: one, the defense would get more intense and work harder to stop me; and two, it would show the coaches the other skills I had that could be used on the field if I wasn't going to be the starting safety. One way or another, I was going to be on the field my sophomore year.

I had a good camp and I felt comfortable and confident with my abilities and my knowledge of the position. I had worked my way up to alternating with Glenn at the safety position with the blue team, but officially remained the starting safety for the red team. But now that camp was over, and I had moved closer to my goal of starting, it was time for Coach Gilbride to make his decision on who would be the starting safety for the first game. Usually, any personnel changes that had to be made were made during that Monday or Tuesday of the week of that upcoming game. I had a few days to relax as everyone either went home for the weekend or moved into their dorm rooms. I decided to move into my dorm room. I didn't have money to go back and forth, and Big Melvin and Sonny weren't planning on going home either. As I lay in my new dorm room on Saturday and Sunday, I wondered what Coach Gilbride's decision would be. I did everything I could to be a starter. Was I still one of the Super Freshman or would I be the second-team safety again and have to wait another year to be a starter? Well, Monday came, and I was feeling anxious as I got dressed for practice. As we went through our position drills and warmups, I could sense in Glenn's interaction with me that he, too, was anxious as to whether he would be keeping his starting position. He made little comments that made me believe he knew something I didn't know and that he was trying to get information out of me—like I knew who would be starting the first game. Well, Monday's practice passed, and Glenn was on the starting blue team defense and I would come in on nickel defense, which added an additional safety to the defense. As normal, I had a very good practice, flying around the field, making hits, and making plays; and most importantly, making the right defensive calls. Glenn was making plays as well, but at times, it appeared he was getting to the play late. I thought he was just jogging to the end of the play because he knew the play was over, but something was off by his play and I couldn't get a handle on what it was. Tuesday's practice was the same. But Wednesday was technically the last day of Coach's evaluation before he would officially determine who would be the starter for the first game. Thursdays were just shoulder pads and helmet days, reviewing the coverages and implementing the special team play: extra point kicking, punt team punt, and punt return teams. I was on the kickoff and punt cover team, so I knew I would be in the game; but that wasn't enough, I needed to be in the entire game because I was the better player. Wednesday's practice went well. I tried even harder this practice because it was my last chance to make an impression on the coaches. At the end of practice when we entered the locker room, we found the starting lineups for the first week's game on the wall. I was not starting. I was disappointed and felt that I was cheated. Sonny came up to me and said, "Don't worry." He, too, thought I had earned my way to the starting position; but he always had a positive attitude and told me to keep my head up and be ready. He said Coach Gilbride would always ready to pull someone from the game if they weren't playing up to their potential or were costing us the game; so, he told me, "Be ready. He can call you at any time." I took that advice and tried to remain positive for the next two days before Opening Day against East Stroudsburg University.

Southern's first game that year was away against East Stroudsburg University, located out in Western Pennsylvania. It was my first time in Pennsylvania other than visiting cousin Clive in Pittsburgh while still in high school. I was anxious because many things, including my future at Southern, were at stake in this game and I knew I had to do something special, or something had to happen that would get me on the field full-time.

Right before the game, the team always said the Lord's Prayer. It was a time to reflect on the purpose of competition, and a moment to exhale and relax a bit from being so excited before we ran out on to the field. After the prayer, I went to the side and prayed again—a more personal prayer to God for guidance and strength to keep my head ready to make the right calls if asked to make them. I wouldn't know if the opportunity would present itself for me to be in that position, but either way, with the Lord on my side, I couldn't go wrong. I recall East Stroudsburg as being hard-hitting and equal in size if not bigger than us. There were no spectacular lays that I can remember, but there was one play that caused us the opportunity to win the game. Glenn was at the safety position on a particular play, lined up on the same side as Sonny, who was playing the strong corner position. A pass was thrown to their side of the field. The ball was underthrown, and Sonny had a beat on the ball. As he was about to intercept the pass, Glenn came out of nowhere and ran into Sonny, which knocked him off the path to intercept the throw. The ball was clearly going to be intercepted, and to see that missed opportunity not only had us all pondering what Glenn was thinking about, but what did he see or not see to have hit Sonny and not intercept the ball himself. It left us puzzled and Coach Gilbride upset. One of the funniest observations as part of being on Southern's football team was to watch Coach Gilbride's responses to ill-informed play and mental mistakes. He had very little patience for players who made mental mistakes that unnecessarily caused us to lose the game, but he knew that too many mistakes would come back and haunt your team later if you were not careful. Well, that play was Glenn's first mistake that eventually cost us the game. East Stroudsburg's receiver caught the ball and they eventually went on to score. Mistakes like that would not be Glenn's last, but his last as the starting free safety. We lost that game 17-14. The beginning of the season didn't start too well. We were 0-1 and heading to an inner-conference foe, Springfield College. After Saturday games, we would return to campus and review game film Sunday night in the field house as a team. The room went silent as that particular play played across the screen. One could hear rumbling in the back of the room by the upperclassmen, which was quickly shut down by Coach Gilbride. Coach Gilbride didn't miss anything on the field. He knew every position, what to do, how many steps it would take, and what angles to take to get a player there. One could tell in his voice that not only was he disappointed, he was also frustrated. Based on what I was sensing in the meeting, I thought that this Wednesday's practice would possibly have a different outcome and that I would be given my opportunity to start.

After the meeting, Glenn knew his time at free safety would be short. He had doubts in his own ability to make plays and knew that Coach Gilbride had a short leash for players who could not fulfill his expectations. Monday's practice was the usual: shorts, helmets, shoulder pads, and review. Tuesday and Wednesday were full contact and intense days that challenged everyone to perform their best. I had a good week of practice, mainly because I believed I would get the call that week to step in as the starter because I now understood the defense, was making all the right calls, and lastly, was intentionally bringing the heat to the upperclassmen when I hit them. I knew in my own head that that week would be my week. After Wednesday practice, I was hoping to see my name on the starting lineup posted on the locker room wall. There was no list. Coach Dodge, the defensive backs coach, came through the locker room and let us now that the list would be up tomorrow during the day and that Coach had to make some changes. That announcement had me feeling more optimistic that one of those changes would be me replacing Glenn as free safety, and now two of the Super Freshman would be playing together making history at Southern. Sonny and a few of the other AA ball players supported me and thought I should be playing too. They believed they could trust me and that I would fit in with the team's personality. Sonny once said, "Pat, you have all the tools; you just need to know how and when to use them." I believed I had grown from my freshman year. But it was obvious that I had much more to learn if I wanted to be champion. Thursday came, and I was anxious to get over to the gym to see if my name was posted as the starting safety. But first, I had to head over to the fine arts building and work on my play. I was a theatre major at first because I wanted to be an actor and model after graduation. My nickname in high school was "Hollywood" because of my animation on the field and from being in high school fashion shows. I really never thought of anything other than that. Myself and another AA male actor were the only ones in the theatre department. The other student was Michael Jai White. That's right—the famous Michael Jai White from Spawn, Tyler Perry, and martial arts movies. He and I did plays by Shakespeare and The River Niger. It was a great experience and I had hoped to be on television one way or another. After theatre class, I headed over to the field house locker room to see the list. There was the usual crowd of players surrounding the board looking for their names. The usual starters usually walked on by and watched the lowerclassmen search in suspense to see if their names were there. I was one of them. As I got closer to the board, I was able to see the lineups of the starting defense. Sonny, Rick, Wade, and Glenn Ricky were the names I saw. I was disappointed and angry that my name wasn't there. I did all that was asked of me; and Glenn made mistakes that put us in difficult positions to win the last game. So, what was the reason for me not getting my chance to start? That decision by Coach Gilbride not to start me stayed with me for the rest of the season, which left a fiery passion in my spirit that if and when I got on the field again, whoever I was up against would feel the hurt that I was feeling. I was a man on a mission!

Wednesday was the last day of full-contact for the week; I made it my goal to hit extra hard with extra intensity and intention. I was angry again, to the point where I couldn't hold it back. My hits that day came with a little more hate and un-forgiveness. The underclassmen that were running scout team unfortunately received a lot of my anger—and a few individuals left the field with assistance. I believed I was the best safety out there and not playing left a nasty taste in my mouth. I believed that Coach Gilbride didn't like me, he didn't trust me, or even that he favored Glenn over me because he was white! My mind wondered and searched for any explanation for why I didn't get the starting position against Springfield. There were a few players that looked at me and shrugged their shoulders as if to also ask why I didn't get to start, but it was game week and the team had to come together if we were to revenge our first loss. Thursday's practice went as usual: helmets, shoulder pads, and review. I knew my responsibilities and made all the right calls when the red group was called out to review coverages and responsibilities. Sonny would give me the nod when I got the calls right and even helped me to make the calls, but I didn't need his help anymore. I had gained confidence in the position and was eager to prove myself as a starter. Sonny would say, "Stay focused. Your time will come. Just be ready." I was ready and more focused than ever; I just needed Coach to give me a chance.

The Springfield game was away and at night. Up until this time in my football experiences, I had only played in one night game, and that was back in Pop Warner when we played a team from Charlotte, North Carolina. The fact that it was a night game added to the excitement of the moment and to my frustration of not being out there as the starter. The game was away, and I was on the kickoff team. I remember running down with a head of steam ready to collide with anyone who was in my way. The ball was returned to the other side of the field, denying me the opportunity to be in on the play. I looked at every play as an opportunity to have Coach notice me and see that I was ready to play immediately! The game was a tight one. The defenses for both teams were playing at their highest. I recall Southern being up by four points going into the fourth quarter with a score of 14-10. I was resigned to the fact that I would not get in as the new safety or get an opportunity to be part of the blue defense. The score was too close, and I believed Coach Gilbride didn't want to take a chance on me in such an important moment in the game; however, God has plans that man doesn't plan for. It might have been second or third down, early in the fourth quarter, and Springfield was driving down the field. They may have been on their own forty-five yard line when the quarterback hiked the ball and was looking for a receiver down the right side of the field. That was Sonny's side, so I felt comfortable that Sonny had his side under control and that a play would be made. As the quarterback let the pass go along the sidelines, Sonny turned towards the field and ran side by side with the receiver. Sonny, again, had zeroed in on the ball and was about to make the interception. We all saw it coming, when out of nowhere, Glenn came over from the hash mark from his safety position attempting to make a play on the ball, and instead of intercepting the ball or hitting the receiver, ran into Sonny, knocking Sonny off the ball and allowing the receiver to catch the ball and run into the end zone for a touchdown. I think everyone's mouth fell open and a loud "oh" came from the sidelines. It was déjà vu. Coach Gilbride was as red as Santa Claus' suit on Christmas morning. You could see that he was on the headphones talking to the assistant coaches attempting to find out what happened on the play. I guess he didn't like what he heard, because I was asked to pick up the headphones and talk to Coach Dodge, who was located in the coaches' booth.

He told me, "You're in. Are you ready?"

I said, "Yes."

And he said, "Go get it."

I did. My time had come, and I was more than ready to play, but I was even angrier than ever. I was angry that the coaches made the decision not to start me, and I believed that if they had put me in earlier or started me, that touchdown never would have happened. Either the ball would have been intercepted by Sonny and I would have knocked him out, or the receiver would have attempted to catch the ball and I would have knocked it loose, or I would have intercepted the ball myself. Either way, that receiver was not going to catch the ball in front of me, and he definitely was not going to score on my side of the field. That is the mentality I had for the game. I took the position that I was the best, despite of my lack size. My drive, determination, and confidence made up for what I was lacking. For the rest of the game, I made the right calls and made good hits that solidified Coach Gilbride's confidence in me. Unfortunately, it was too little too late, because we lost. I wanted that win for us and especially for him.

We were now 0-2; not the way we wanted to begin the season. With me in the starting rotation, the current losing streak would now end. We went through the rest of the season playing much better. We beat American International the following week 37-14, and I picked off my first pass. It was a relief to get that the first one under my belt as I was greeted by my teammates with cheers and hugs. Coach Gilbride didn't say much after a player did something good. It's like he expected it from a player. It was like he saw things that that the rest of us didn't as a coach; he had that sense of what it took to bring the best out of a player. We got our record up to 4-2 before going into one of my best games as a sophomore. We had beat AIC, Cheney U, and Kutztown. We were about to face UDC, The University of District of Colombia. UDC was a HBCU (Historically Black College and University) in Washington, DC. The players were from the South. They were big and fast. I was initially intimidated by their size when they first walked on the field and were warming up. I looked over to their sidelines to view the receivers and their speed as they ran their warm-up drills. One thing is for sure, "You can't judge a book by its cover." Although they were big, they didn't play big, and they didn't play as a unit.

One thing Gilbride preached all the time was that, "We are a team and there are no individual superstars on our team." It was a cold, rainy day at our home field. Bowen Field was old and run down. There was very little grass and the rain turned what was left into inches of mud and mud puddles. In spite of the conditions, we came to play, and just like the year before out in California, we were about to show another geographical corner of America that we play ball at Southern Connecticut. We rumbled through the UDC offense, racking up yardage on the ground. Our big feature fullback out of the wing T, Bill Clancy, ran over their defense like they were there on a sunny Sunday afternoon. On defense, UDC didn't fare much better. Their quarterback was sacked in the end zone where I happened to be, and I fell on it for a touchdown. That was my first college touchdown and I was psyched. With my first opportunity to play, I didn't disappoint Coach Gilbride or myself. I know if I were to mess up, the long arm of the hook was ready to pull me out. I wasn't done yet, however. We solidified our win in the third quarter with UDC down by thirty points. They started to drive down the field, when the quarterback dropped back to throw the ball towards my side of the field. I was playing cover three, in the middle of the field when he threw it towards a receiver; I stepped in front and galloped in the mud, slashing my way forward towards the end zone. It felt like forever to get there due to the conditions of the field. I did finally get there, seventy-two yards later as I dove across the goal line before a UDC player attempted to knock my legs from underneath me. I was tired, as Rick and Sonny jumped on me and congratulated me. It was a great feeling to know I could contribute to a win, as well as win the confidence of my teammates. We beat UDC 59-0. We only lost one other game that year in 1984; it was to the University of Indiana of Pennsylvania—at that time a Division II Powerhouse. The future looked good for Southern football; two of the Super Freshmen were now on the field and the other underclassmen were playing well—and under Coach Gilbride's leadership, the future was promising.

Chapter Eight

Building Blocks

It was shocking and disappointing when I found out Coach Gilbride was leaving Southern Connecticut. He decided to leave Southern to pursue professional opportunities in the Canadian Football League. I felt like I lost part of my identity and masculinity when he left. Before him, I lived life recklessly and without order. Under his guidance and tutelage, I was being groomed, not just to be a great football player, but also to be a better man. During this time back home in New Rochelle, my mother was still having issues with my stepfather and his constant drinking, volatile behavior, and inappropriate social activities. My life under Coach Gilbride provided me with a refuge of solace, a barometer of manhood, and discipline and strength to help me maintain a level mental stability during this time of uncertainty at home. Now that Coach was gone, along with Sonny, Wade, and Mike West, who graduated that year, and Travis Tucker, who was drafted to the NFL, the blanket of support and encouragement and accountability was no longer a locker stall away. I had to assess my place on the team and what I had to offer for its future success. These young men went through the trials and fire under Coach Gilbride to build the program into what it had become, and they transferred what they had learned over the years to me; I was grateful for it, but now they were all gone! I even learned from Glenn Ricky, but he was gone as well. I was now expected to be one of the leaders of the team. There was Ricky, a veteran now after playing consistently for the past two years, and myself, who had been thrown into the fire the previous year by default. We also had new faces that would definitely impact what we were up against this coming season. There were new faces like Mathew Morrow, who was now eligible to play after transferring from Virginia State, Jeff Smith, who also was from New Ro and showing promise that he was ready to step up and be an impact player while alternating with senior, David Henley. There were also some up-and-coming, impressive sophomores like Glenn Kimbrough, from Queens, New York, and John Harris, from Spring Valley, New York. The forthcoming year and future seemed promising and uncertain at that same time. The question remained in my mind—and I believe in the minds of others from teammates to coaches—Would I be ready to take on the role as one of the leaders of the team, and the leader of the defensive backfield? I didn't have time to think about it because my time had come and there was no one else ready or available to fill the position. There were recruits that had come in generating rumors about their size and proposed hitting ability and that they would be challenging me for the safety position. I wasn't worried about that, and in fact, that motivated me and elevated my level of determination even more, as would soon be demonstrated during training camp in August 1985.

Camp started the same way it had begun the two years before. We checked into our dorms and then headed over to the field house for a team meeting. We were joking around before the coaches came in, caught up with each other about our summer adventures, and assessed who came back bigger and stronger. A few noticeable changes were with Scott Measereau. As a freshman, he was about two hundred and fifteen pounds; but now as a junior, he was at least two-sixty. Our linebackers, Bob Gibson and Matt Mclees, also got bigger and stronger than the year before. I believed the coming year would be an exciting one because we had players who gained some playing time the year before and who had the ability to play, as well as worked hard over the summer to prepare for the upcoming season. The only concern I had moving forward was that we were going to be a young defense and whether this young defense would have enough to overcome our overall inexperience.

The year started off pretty rough for me. I was not allowed back into the resident dorms because I was not following dormitory rules the year before. Nothing really serious—but not attending meetings, having overnight without signing in, and a few verbal confrontations with dorm director about these concerns left him no other choice but to not allow me return. I was not notified over the summer, which would have at least given me the opportunity to look for an alternative living situation before the year would have begun. I was forced to ramp up my search for housing for my junior year. Interesting and thankfully, I wasn't the only one in this predicament. There were other teammates who happened to be in the same position and were looking for housing too. This provided extra eyes on the streets looking for housing which took the pressure off of me. I ended sharing an apartment with Glenn, Matt, J.C. (our senior running back), and John. The school year was just about to begin, and much of the local housing around the school was taken by the time we had started and eventually found something. So in between practices, we made phone calls to local housing units with the hope of obtaining one before the school year began. I had to tell Kandice what my dilemma was, and fortunately for me, she was willing to offer her family's home to me if I needed it. I met her at the end of my sophomore year. Her name was Kandice Jones, a "townie." That's what college students called the residence of the city or town that the school is located in. I met her after a game on my way to a celebration party at an off-campus apartment. The party was being held by one of the upperclassman's apartments, where there were kegs of beer, players, women, and more kegs of beer. I wasn't a drinker anymore after having had negative experiences dating back to high school, at home, as well as some incidences while living in the dorms; so, I indulged sparingly. She was with her cousins (that I found out later) out on the town that night and was invited by the upperclassmen she knew. I attempted to talk to her with my savoir-faire lines as we both were heading in the same direction of the party house, as much as a young, testosterone-filled young man could. She wasn't going for it. She actually looked at her cousins, then at me, as though I was crazy for attempting to talk to her in the first place. I quietly stepped away as I followed her into the party as we went our separate ways. Through some perseverance, Kandice and her family would be a very important resource and support for me while in school. Kandice didn't initially believe I played football based on my physical stature. The upperclassmen she new—Van Clive, Big Melvin, and others—were big impressive men, so when she saw me, she thought I was joking that I played football for Southern and that I was just trying to get close to her. Kandice and her family were very supportive of me my junior year and, because of them, allowed me to have the best season of my collegiate career.

School was becoming a little more intense and demanding along with my training. The financial resources would change and be even more limited which carried an additional burden on my mind that year too. After two years, my weight hadn't moved much. I was still only one hundred and eighty pounds going into my junior year, and everyone around me was getting bigger and stronger. Going into the season, I made an effort to maintain my weight and stay eligible.

Camp was one week away, and we had not yet secured housing for the up-coming year. We ramped up our search all over New Haven and being in close vicinity of the school was no longer part of the criteria. We eventually found an apartment about three miles away from campus. Glenn had a car, so we believed if it came down to it, we could always get a ride to and from school and home after practice and games. The apartment was located on the outskirts of downtown New Haven, on the other side of Yale University. The walk in the mornings would be a trek, and harsh in the winter for us, but we didn't have a choice. I knew that if there were nights where I was too tired to walk home, I could always stay at Kandice's house. The question now was how I would pay for it.

I was waiting for my financial aid to come in, but until then I needed to provide my share of the deposit. I didn't have any money. I asked mom for three hundred dollars, but she didn't have it either. I reluctantly went to Coach Cavanaugh and told him the situation. I really didn't want to, but I was desperate and needed somewhere to live. Before practice the next day, I went into Coach Cavanaugh's office and told him who I was living with and where. He asked a bunch of questions, like why so far and if the other guys were in the same situation.

After about a half-hour of consultation, Coach Cavanaugh said, "Come by tomorrow and I'll give you the deposit, and don't worry about paying me back." Not sure why he said not to worry about paying him back, because it was always my intention to do so. My housing was now set and I was able to concentrate on school and football.

Closing out the previous year, I ended the season with two interceptions—one of them being returned for a seventy-five-yard touchdown. I had forty solo tackles and one fumble recovery for another touchdown. Going into my junior year, I planned to top that. The defense was ready, including Matt, who had solidified his way into the starting lineup after a great spring game where he collected four interceptions—beating out an upperclassman at the left cornerback position. I would be the starting free safety, Smitty at strong safety, and Rick (California Boy) held down the right cornerback position. The defensive backfield was ready to go, but we were still left with some concerns with both defensive and offensive front lines. In the previous years, the front lines were held down by a special group of veterans who were personally sorted out and recruited out of high school by Coach Gilbride. That group and their backups had now graduated, and the more inexperienced backups to the backups the year before would now be on the "front lines," given the opportunity to play; whether they had been paying attention in practice and on the sidelines for those first two years would now be on display. The only players I recall that had gotten significant playing time the year before was Scott Mersereau, Glen Magyar, a six-foot-six, two-hundred-and-sixty-pound tackle who played opposite to Scott and Rick. A force on the defensive line would make a significant impact on our success, indeed, but more manpower would be needed for us to be successful as a whole.

The season didn't go as we would have liked. Yes, we were young, but we were also a team of fighters and winners who were not used to losing. As a matter of fact, we started the season 3-0 and were looking to improve as we approached the "meat" of the schedule. Our cross-town rival, Central Connecticut and West Haven Division II powerhouse, University of New Haven, was always battle.

Central was a team that wasn't necessarily better than Southern, but over the years as competing State Schools, the two teams recruited and competed for the same players from the same geographical areas, and New Ro was one of them. My high school teammate at defensive end in high school, Hubert Parris, had transferred to Central from New York Tech. Rob Castagna, my high school captain, was playing nose tackle for Central. So, it was more than just a game that day; it was also a question of who had made the right decision on where to play football. Although Central was a critical appointment, the first Big game would come when we played the University of New Haven (UNH), a Division II power, that also provided financial athletic scholarships to its players—contrary to Southern who provided financial aid to help its players out. That game would bring out the local newspaper writers, media, and draw a crowd of three to five thousand people, which was a lot for a Division II game in the northeastern part of the United States. Like always, it was a close game. It was one of those games where if I was going to grow and demonstrate leadership and maturity, this would be the game to begin. The first thing I did was pick of the pass of UNH's star quarterback, Paul Kelly, as they moved down the field. We also felt empowered as we watched our offense move the ball down the field with precision against their stud defense. The offense finally scored, bringing the score to 13-10, UNH. We were now in striking distance to make a move. There's a saying in football, "defense wins games," and as I looked into the eyes of our defense, I could see the intensity and hunger for this win. We were on the cusp of moving up the national rankings if we could win this one. UNH was set to drive towards our end zone and score again. Something had to happen, and the defense would have to step up with less than seven minutes left in the game. The ball was inside our forty-five-yard line and one could feel the tension in the air that something was about to happen. As Paul Kelly dropped back to throw a pass, one could see that he had one intention and that was to hit his number one receiver coming across on a slant route. I picked up his read and aiming point as I broke on a forty-five-degree angle towards the aiming point where he wanted to throw the ball. It felt like I was running in slow motion as I intercepted the ball! I legged it sixty-four yards and pointing my way towards the end zone along the right sideline. One of the animations I'm known for is having a white towel hanging from my pant waistline. The towel blew in the wind as I ran as fast as I could, pointing towards the other end zone, which begun at the forty-yard line. This play, in less than three minutes, put us ahead 17-13. After we kicked off to them, our defense held them again by a great play by our linebacker Ron Williams, known as the "Reaper." He was called the Reaper because of his dark persona and dark and quiet demeanor. He was a terror as our inside line-backer that could be depended on most of the time; and this was one of those times. I mentioned earlier that I felt something was in the air, and I was right. The ball was punted back to us and the offense stalled with less than two minutes left in the game. As the end of the game grew close to the end, it was evident that the outcome would not be determined to until the last tick of the clock. After a few plays and now with one minute left in the game, on fourth and twelve, UHN had the ball on the eighteen-yard line when Paul Kelly found his number one receiver on the eight-yard line. We were all in shock because we knew the game wouldn't be over until it was over. With less than one minute left in the game and with a new set of downs, that one-minute felt like an eternity. So, from the eight-yard line, UNH attempted to run the ball down our throat. Our defense held for the first two runs. I think they believed they could try it again, so we buckled in and were ready. This time, it was a play-action play that was an attempt to draw the linebackers and defensive backs up, leaving the secondary vulnerable to the pass. It worked! Although our senior nose tackle, Buckley, had made it through his blocker and was on Kelly's heals, Kelly was able to get the pass off and towards his intended receiver. As the ball float in the air over my head, it felt like all the noise from the crowd had gone mute. I couldn't hear a sound and my head was in a fog as I witnessed the ball fall into the hands of the opposing player. We were in man coverage and my receiver, the tight end, stayed in to add additional protection for Kelly—who left me stuck near the line of scrimmage and unable to be involved in the play for fear my player would go out late for a pass. I was crushed! Our season was now in jeopardy as the time ran out during our attempt to razzle-and-dazzle the ball down the field of the ensuing kickoff. The feeling of despair and disappointment would remain in the air for the rest of the season as we lost a few more games and ended up with a 4-5 record. To this day, I remember the UNH's motto, "a team that won't be beat, can't be beat," as time ran out, losing 20-17.

The 1985 season taught me much about winning and losing. Personally, although the season ended up being my best season numerically in my college career and solidified me as a candidate for the National Football League, it was also a disappointing one from a team perspective, which fell well short of its goals and aspirations to have a winning record. It felt like we let down the university—a university with a long history of success within its athletic programs. However, we never felt that feeling from the student body. Four of the five games we lost, we lost by less than three points. Our effort was there but we fell short. Our friends were always encouraging and recognized our efforts on the field were one hundred percent. Although we ended up with four wins and five losses—the worst record in six years—we would take that support and encouragement and use it as we finished out the season, looking forward to our senior year, 1986.

In 1986, I planned to do more than I had done any other year while at Southern. By now, Kandice and I were full swing in a relationship, and her family offered their home over the summer so I could focus and train at the school. My mother saved up some money and bought about thirty steaks to eat over the summer with potatoes. I ran as much as I could while working on my technique and agility. I would run through West Rock Mountain through a running path that begun near Kandice's house and ended up down below two blocks away from campus. That summer all I did was lift weights and eat steak and potatoes. Kandice did her best to keep up with me as she went running with me sometimes through West Rock for added support as I ran hills for additional strength training. I did everything I could to prepare for the upcoming season because I knew my teammates would be doing the same thing wherever they were. When camp started in August of 1986, I was shocked with delight as I witnessed my teammates pull up in front of the dorms in cars with different license plates representing the many states my teammates came from. Scott had grown into a massive mound of strength. He weighed in at 285 pounds and 6 3″. Rick (California Boy) weighed more than me at 185 pounds. Linebackers Matt Mclees and Bob Gibson looked like something out of the old Pittsburgh Steelers. When I asked Scott and some of the other linemen, who decided to stay around for the summer, what they ate, they said they ate a lot of peanut butter and jelly and lifted weights. I felt like I wasted my mother's money because, although I was in great shape, my weight only went up five pounds to 185 pounds. The guys looked ready for the upcoming season and appeared mentally and physically prepared to take on the all appointments.

The 1986 season began the same way the 1985 season ended, with a loss! We lost to Kutztown University—the same university where we had some racial tensions the year before. It was heartbreaking and had me rethinking our potential future. Coach Cavanaugh brought us together and reminded us of our greatness, ability, and potential as seniors: We must lean on our history, the spirit of the past players, and the lessons of winning passed down to us from previous Southern players. I immediately thought of those guys: Sonny, Big B, Melvin Wells, Van Clive, Travis Tucker, and Stoutland. These players lost some, but they never gave up. They took their losses out on the next appointment and practiced that week with passion and purpose. We took to the practice field that week with a mission to be better and practice with intention. I felt sorry for the scout teams that gave us a look that week. Our defense had new life and whoever was in our way would feel the heat of that passion.

Next up on the schedule was Cheyney State University, a Historical Black University in Pennsylvania that had a mediocre record but always had good skill and big players that could beat any team on any given day. I recall the day to be gloomy, cloudy, and wet. The Chaney team was big as expected, with an exceptional tight end that stood 6 3″ and 220 pounds. He had good size and speed, and the scouting report on him was that he would be a major target for Cheyney for them to have any chance to win the game. I kept him in the back of my mind by keeping a close tab on him, hitting him whenever and wherever I could, even if he didn't have the ball. I had a dominating game against Cheyney! I had a few pass breakups and major hits, stopping first downs and laying some major hits on their team. I was even able to dislodge one pass attempt to the tight end coming across the middle. This was our first win of the season and we took it with pride and as the beginning to a new chapter in Southern football and my career.

Next up was Springfield College. As a sophomore, it was the turning point in my college career after replacing Glenn Ricky at safety and ending the air assault on our defensive backfield. As a senior, I told my self that we would not lose to Springfield College again; not because I was in the secondary, but because of the men that supported me in what I do at the free safety position. Our current defense was now one that grew together as emerging teammates and potential starters since sophomore year. Literally, me, Matt, and Smitty started this journey four years earlier to make this the best experience of our football lives. This attitude and approach is what we took into every game as seniors and juniors knowing that as quickly as our careers had begun with high hopes and dreams, would also come to a screeching end in a few short weeks. Springfield College was in our path to writing our own goodbye story and unfortunately for them, we were coming through Springfield, Massachusetts with a band of fighting Owls to complete the narrative with an exclamation. It was a perfect September night in Springfield, Massachusetts. It was comfortably warm under the football lights of Benedum Field. Southern didn't have facilities that would allow us to play football at night and we didn't have our own field. We played at the city-owned filed where the local high school, Hill House, played; at a field that had endured over the past 100 years as it stood there in the belly of New Haven, Connecticut. You could tell at one time Hill House and its field stood as a centerpiece of sports in the New Haven community with Hall of Fame players like Walter Camp, Dr. James Naismith, Floyd Little, and State Supreme Court Justice, Constance Motley. The architectural structure of the stadium mirrored classic Roman cement seating with crumbling morter barely holding it in place in 1986. Unfortunately, over years, due to fiscal issues and the fast pace of technology, Bowen Field had been left behind and not been considered an "attractive" place to play. But it was our field, our home, and we made the best of what we had. In today's times, what a school's facility has to offer and what it looks like plays a great deal on whether a student athlete will attend the school or not—missing the blessings that may be offered to them right in the face. Our senior class was promised a new field during our recruiting process and was approved, ready for games on campus by our sophomore year. Well, it never happened, and we didn't miss it; we grew stronger as a team because of it. We played through dry dust patches on the legendary field and learned to "brush it off," playing hard, dirty football that would challenge us as players and as men. Stepping on the field in Springfield was like playing on a professional football field to us. It excited us even more knowing this would be the only time this season that we would get to play on an artificial turf and we made the best of it. I took pride in my hitting ability due to being undersized at the free safety position. So, every time I went out onto the field, it was my objective to give my all on every play; that included hitting as hard, running as fast as I could, and of course, remembering the coverages. My performance that night reinforced that position and unfortunately for two Springfield players, there evening ended early due to the crushing hits I laid on them that evening as we won the game 37-14. We were on a roll now with aspirations of having an impactful season to be remembered by the senior class.

We were on a winning streak that put our record at 4-1 going into one of the most anticipated games of the year with an out-of-conference, top-tier challenge with Liberty Baptist University, located in Lynchburg, Virginia. Jerry Farwell, the founder and president of the school, created a southern evangelical coeducational university for Christians to play sports and to groom young people with the moral and spiritual Christian values. They also provided scholarship money for their student body, which allowed them to recruit very good athletes from across the country. They had two main players: Wayne Haddix (who became my roommate with the Giants), defensive back, and Eric Green, a massive, six-foot-five, two-hundred-and-seventy-pound tight end who had NFL teams looking at them. By now the word had gotten out that I too was being looked at by NFL Scouts as a potential player; and media conversation was who would out perform whom in this contest of potential professional players. I took the match up as a challenge, because I knew a lot of schools underestimated Southern football and its ability to compete with top-tier teams, as well as personally proving that I could play here and anywhere else if allowed to. As always, I looked to something that I could use to motivate me to perform at my highest level. The game at Liberty provided that motivation that I used for that game, and to this day it still remains in my memory. I don't know for sure in 1986 or if there is a policy currently in place in 2017, but I understand that there was something in place in 1986 that I used to re-direct my rage to confront in my eyes an injustice.

Pop Warner Youth Tackle developed many young men into becoming great football players and students. One player from those early Pop Warner days who I played with on the Chiefs was McCutcheon He played on the defensive line due to his size and his ability to move for a child of his size and hit with force and intention. Unfortunately, he and his family moved away from New Rochelle to Virginia before junior high and many of us who played with him were disappointed about his family's move because he was good, and he would have added to the great defense when heading to the high school. At the time we were disappointed, but we moved on as children do. Well as God had planned it, I was informed by Joe Fosina, while home over the summer in New Rochelle, that McCouchen was attending Liberty Baptist in Lynchburg, Virginia. He didn't say he was playing, he said he was "attending." I was anxious to see him when I looked at the roster during our Monday meetings reviewing the opponent's personnel. However, when we arrived in Virginia by Thursday night, I learned that McChuachen, who is black, was kicked of the team. The violation was that he violated school policy of either interracial dating or showing affection in public with a fellow student who was white. It was disappointing and unsettling not seeing him—conjuring up anger knowing he was kicked out of school for this alleged offense. This news brought back memories of previous racial tension on the field while playing college football, and I used this revelation as motivation for the game. This new revelation brought out the tempered anger that once steered and intensified my passion on the field and the distaste for those who embraced such a policy or unwritten position by the school. It was hard for me to understand that racism and sports was still so active in 1986. My eyes were opened that day when I stepped onto the field and the rumors were confirmed when I saw that McCouchen wasn't there.

Eric Green was an imposing figure on the field and I would be the one who, from the safety position, would have multiple opportunities to cover him. Because of his position, most times the tight end and safety usually are the ones coming face-to-face because of the routes that are ran by that position, which usually are within the area of the free safety's responsibility. As we expected, the game was a hard fought one and we did play to our potential and ability because Liberty was precise in their execution of plays and operated like a well-oiled machine. In the fourth quarter heading towards the end of the game, we were ahead by the score of 27 to 21 after a three-yard run by John Harris—the other half of our running back duo. Glenn had racked up over 130 yards that game and with his last carries had brought the ball once again into scoring range. Unfortunately, our offense stumbled and wasn't able to score and put the game away for good. There was still time remaining on the clock and Liberty was heading to our end zone after short passes and running plays. In the back of my mind, I said to myself, "We've come a long way and we are not going home as losers."

As Liberty approached the twenty-yard line, I knew they would seek out Mr. Green at some point as their main target going down the stretch for the big play. I was right, and on third down, with less than two minutes to ago, the Liberty quarterback decided to throw the ball in the direction of big Eric Green. I remember he took an outside release off the line to throw me off as if he was running an outside route, but he readjusted his pattern and headed up the hash mark towards me. I was lined up over the opposite side guard in the center of the field in a cover-three look. I took my three read steps (steps that would tell me if it was a running play or pass play), the quarterback gave a run read, which told me to come up and help out on the run play. As I reacted to the read, I saw Eric Green heading up the seam and looking back for the ball; I realized that it wasn't a run at all and that the play action was to throw me off and put me out of position to make a play. I reacted immediately and headed towards the hash mark directly at the big tight end. I knew the Liberty quarterback would be looking for his number one receiver for the tie and possible win. The ball was thrown to him as he maneuvered his massive body and raised his hands to catch the ball. As his hands touched the ball I thought to myself that this couldn't be happening, as I saw his massive hands reach up and grasp at the ball. I was one step away, which meant I lost the opportunity to intercept the ball, but I was still one step closer with a chance to stop him from completely grasping the ball and scoring. As his fingers reached around and secured the ball, he turned his body around to head up field holding onto the ball with both hands. At that very instant I laid the most furious and devastating hit that I have ever landed on an opponent in my college football career! The ball flew out of the tight end's hands as the ball was dislodged and landed on the ground; and his body flew and twisted in a hundred-and-eighty-degree turn. As my head cleared after a few seconds, Eric Green laid there, motionless on the warm, Lynchburg, Virginia grass. He was out—not knocked out, but dazed and unable to gather himself for a few minutes. When I saw that the ball was separated and laid next to him on the grass, I jumped for joy as I saw the referee motion incomplete pass. I was happy no doubt and was about to rejoice and celebrate with my teammates in my attempt to run off the field, when suddenly my left shoulder went numb and a shot of pain shot down my shoulder into my arm and down into my fingers. The pain was so intense that I dropped immediately to my knees. I was now out on my knees in agonizing pain. Both Green and myself were laid out on the field waiting for each team's training staff to reach their new patients. After a few minutes, Green made his way to his feet and headed off the field towards his sidelines. After a couple of minutes my shoulder started to get its feeling back as the blood flowed back to the trauma areas from the big collision. That play sealed the win for Southern as Liberty attempted to go for it on fourth down but failed. The game ended 27-21. The long bus ride home wasn't long enough as we joked, sang songs, and laughed all the way back to New Haven, Connecticut.

I viewed the remainder of the season as a disappointment. We would lose the next two out of four games, losing to University of New Haven again, our cross-town rivals, and the University of Rhode Island. And although URI was a I-AA team, they were 0-8 coming into the game and looking at their roster—man on man—they were not much better than us to not have put up a better performance than we did. It was a rainy, cold day, but no excuse for losing 18-34. This game was the first game I remember where I gave up a touchdown covering a man. I felt I contributed to the loss and to this day it haunts me that I didn't "make the play." We won the last two games beating Central Connecticut 13-0, our crosstown rival, and East Stroudsburg University, 17-0. I guess its perspective on how one views success. I guess it was a successful season, mainly because the prior season we lost five games. I learned to take victories no matter how small, and that in winning and losing there is always something to learn. In a team sport, I've learned I am just one segment in the link of Southern football and that while I was there, I should keep that link in tact for future players to come and strengthen the bond that had kept the program going for over so many years. Our record opened the pathway to Southern's winning ways for future players and teams to build on through Coach Cavanaugh's guidance. That would be the case because Coach Cavanaugh ended his thirty-five-year coaching career with multiple championships under his belt that even Coach Gilbride wasn't able to achieve while at Southern.

I learned a lot about myself that last year. I reflected on the first game I attended in 1983 and how nervous I was getting on the field with some of the best athletes to ever grace the gridiron of Bowen Field—being able to hold my own. I don't know if it was out of fear or out of anger that kept me going mentally through the four years at Southern, but I am thankful to God to have been by my side, holding me up and keeping safe from others and from myself. What was I thinking back then to get myself kicked out of dorms? What was I thinking when I drank so much grain alcohol that I put my health, education, and future at risk? My life at Southern was a good one that I could have thrown because of this lifestyle. Yes, I didn't get to enjoy all the extracurricular activities like other undergraduate students, such as Octoberfest or spring-break vacations like other students. While other undergrads were doing this over spring break, the football team would be sweating in the weight room and working on the dusty grass fields back at Southern Connecticut, getting ready for the spring game. This is the compromise of success that college athletes pay to want to represent their school and reach higher heights other than to graduate from college. I wanted to leave an impact, a standard of commitment; a memory for those that would come after me that when they heard my name, they would say of me, "I represented the school well on the gridiron," and say, "well done." I may have compromised somethings, but I gained so much more by "living the dream."

Chapter Nine

Got Game

My college career was over, and the lingering question was, "What am I going to do now?" I was expecting to receive my diploma in June of 1987, but at the same time I wasn't sure what the future would have in store for me athletically. It would be a few months before the draft and I wouldn't know if my name would be called. The season ended in November, and shortly after that the football office started to receive calls from NFL scouts who wanted to meet me and test me. This was the follow-up to the letters I received right before the beginning of the season. My best time in the forty-yard dash up till then was 4.55. For a safety, that was pretty good, and because of my play on the field for the past two seasons, I believed I put my self in a good position to get a second look. The NFL team that spent the most time with me, coming back twice, was the Los Angeles Raiders. A Raider scout initially came in August of 1986 and looked at film and spoke to Coach Dunne and me awhile. The scout, Angelo Coia, left his card with me and said, "We'll be in touch." I still have to this day. Mr. Coia came back in December to evaluate me and had me run the forty-yard Dash for him; took my height and weight and talked some more. The problem was, each time he came I didn't know he was coming and I wasn't prepared to run. I got a call on the day of his arrival from one of the coaches that "the Raider scout would be here today," and that "he wants you to run for him." I wasn't sure how I felt about it, but I really didn't have a choice but to run. After midday classes that day, I met Mr. Coia in the Moore Field

House, the same place I started my college career, and the same place where I would hopefully impress this scout which would allow me the opportunity to begin another career in the National Football League. As I loosened up and stretched as best as I could, I felt a sense of anxiety come over me. Through my mind ran the thoughts of the possibilities of me being an NFL player and how I could change the lives of my family and my loved ones. I also felt a sense of pressure come over me, which turned my emotions from a place of calm to anxiety. As I readied myself to run the first of two forty-yard dashes, I placed and pressed my fingers along the starting line firmly into the rubber track of the Moorefield House. I heard a voice from the far end of the lane, forty yards away say, "on your movement"; that was Mr. Coia letting me know he was ready for me and that it was time to go. I took a few deep breaths to calm myself, and it helped for just a moment as I felt my heart rate race back up as if I had already ran the race. I raised my body up into the three-point runner's stance and took one last breath in, then out as I shot out from behind the white line of the rubber track. As I ran down the lane, I could feel my legs turn to jelly as the anxiety made its way through my body. I moved as fast as I could, fighting and stretching my body forward as much as I could. As I approached the finish line where scout Coia stood, I accelerated through the line, leaning across and hoping to have ran one of my best times. As I ran through the line and gradually slowed down around the rubber track, I felt a sense of relief but not satisfaction. I knew I didn't run well because my mind and body were not in sink. I was too tense to run, and I felt my time would reflect that. I made my way back to Mr. Coia who had my time waiting for me. He said, "4.67." I was devastated. That was a tenth slower than my best previous times and I knew that would not be good enough to leave an impact. Coming from a Division II School, one's measurables should have been as equal, if not better than, those athletes from the big Power Five schools. So, I knew I hadn't impressed the scout with any of my numbers thus far. However, I had another attempt at it, and this time I would be more relaxed, and think of something to motivate me down the rubber track.

As I prepared to run again, lining up behind the white rubber line that separated me from my destiny, I thought again of those who would be counting on me for my success, along with knowing the first attempt was not my best. As I rose up again in the three-point stance, with my fingers firm, but not pressured along the white line, I felt a different sense of urgency about this run. I was calmer than the first run, but tense with determination and grit to do better than before. "Set. Go!" I said in my head as I shot out from behind the white line. This time I was concentrating and accelerating after thirty yards, trying to find more speed as I got closer and closer to the end line. I dashed across the end line and felt my time this time was better than the first. I still didn't feel comfortable running altogether, but it would be the best for that day, what ever the time would be. As I headed back towards scout Coia, I noticed he was walking towards me, not smiling but not frowning either. He said, "4.61." I was disappointed again, because I knew I could have run faster than two the times I ran for him. I heard that scout's times come up different than high school and college coaches, but I didn't think it would be that much of a difference. That was it for the day. He took my weight, which was 189 pounds, and some body measurements, and he was off. It was a wonderful experience, and although I didn't feel I performed my best, I knew it was an experience that only a few would ever have.

It was time to put much focus on my schoolwork. I was getting through school doing just enough to get by. I was smart, but I wasn't given my all. My time was taken up with drinking, hanging with friends, and spending much of my time with Kandice. Our relationship had grown into a full commitment over the last two years, and we considered moving forward after I got out of Southern. My focus was finishing out my senior year positively and graduating with a degree in corporate communications with a minor in dramatic arts. I felt as the year grew to the end that she thought I was planning to leave her, and because of her uncertainty, our relationship turned from pleasant to contentious. I started to spend more time away with my friends at school and experiencing my last months at school embracing the college experience. My last four years were taken up with football meetings, spring games, fall games, and now, I no longer had those responsibilities. I wanted to be a student for the last five months of my student-athlete days at Southern Connecticut.

I told my mother and stepfather what was going on with me and the possibility of playing on the next level. My mom listened to what I was saying and was excited, but I'm sure she didn't totally understand the gravity of the possibility of me playing in the NFL. Mom was from the islands (Jamaica), and all she new was "big men" that "bump" into one another. She worried all the time about my size and that I wasn't big enough to play. When I told her that scouts and teams were sending me letters at school, she was surprised and asked, "Are you confident enough?" She always asked that, and I wasn't sure how to take it. I always thought Mom didn't think I was good enough in what I did, in spite of my accomplishments. I believe her perspective on sports was secondary to a professional corporate job; and to be successful in America, you need to be good at a traditional professional career as an accountant, lawyer, or doctor. My stepfather, who was doing pretty well at this moment, had reduced his drinking and he and mom were on a good streak. When I told him that I was possibly heading to the pros and that NFL scouts had come to see me, like always, his response in his English sarcastic humor would be, as he kept his eyes locked in the day's newspaper, "Did you play anyone?" Or, "Do they know what they are doing?" Or, "Oh, really." I would even tell him how hard I would hit the opposing players and how they would have to leave the game. His response would be, "Did he really feel it? Or, "Are you sure the guy wasn't just taking a break from the game." Most of his responses were the same, with not much outward encouragement or expression of enthusiasm. But I knew he wanted to know, and I knew he cared, because I can still see him and Mom sitting quietly in the stands watching my every play, "bumping" the opposing team's players.

When I got back to school, my main focus was to finish out my studies to ensure my graduation. I went to the registrar's office to make sure I completed all my class requirements and accumulated enough credits to graduate in June. After going over my transcripts with the register representative, I was informed that I was three credits short of graduation. I was in complete shock and wondered how! Why would they tell me now, at the closing of the school year and me possibly not being around after the draft? There was no way of completing this requirement for my degree by June. I was disappointed and angry again because I was not notified that I was short a class by the team's academic advisor or the registrar's office. And on top of that, the class was Spanish II! When I asked what the mix up was, I was told that when I changed majors my junior year from drama (fine arts) to corporate communications that also changed my degree program from BA to BS. It sure was "BS" and now I had to figure out a way to graduate before the year ended or before the following fall semester would begin. After some research, I was given two options: The first option was to take the class during intercession—which would be like taking a two-week summer class—pass, then graduate. That class would be given during the second half of intersession classes, which would be in July of 1987. I couldn't do it then because by then, I would be in an NFL camp somewhere around the country, and the last thing I wanted to worry about was taking some Spanish test. The second option would be taking the end-of-year test for Spanish II right after the class ended, passing, and my grades would be put in as part of the first intersession class grades. Wow! I thought. Taking the Spanish two tests without ever taking the class? I passed Spanish 100 my sophomore year, but it had been two years since I had passed and by now I thought I had forgotten some of what I had already learned. Those were my two choices, so I went out on faith and chose to take the Spanish II test in May right after the school year ended in hope of passing and not having to come back to campus to finish out school the following Fall.

Well there was no preparation for the test; I just had to go back and review what I learned before and do my best. The test would be in narrative form, which meant, if I was able to put a couple of sentences together, I could possibly pass. I remembered the days, the months, the numbers, and conjugate verbs, so with that in mind with the other, basic Spanish words, I thought I could make it through. I only had to pass, and at this point I didn't care what that number was—sixty-five or eighty-five percent—just passing was the goal. The test would be held in one of the lecture halls in the Engelman Building. As I sat there, my nerves started to work on me again, thinking about how important it was for me to pass this test—another thing to worry about outside of football before my career even got started. I'm not sure if the pressure was self-imposed or if it was that I didn't want to return home that summer and face my mother without my degree in hand. My mother never finished high school and only one person in my extended family at the time had attended college and that was Clive. My cousins, who lived in Brooklyn, had moved to the United States from Jamaica; they had finished high school in the United States but after high school went into the Army. So, I would be the first in my immediate family and second in our entire family to graduate from college. As I sat there waiting for the test to be handed out, these many thoughts were running through my head. The blue textbooks were handed out with stapled, typed instructions written on it, along with a scenario to be translated and responded to. I got to it and worked my way through the test, recalling on as much Spanish as I could muster up from sophomore year. "Como si llama usted, mi llama Patricio Senior!" As I worked my way through the translation, after an hour and a half of focus and recall, I was all done. I did the best I could, and whatever was going to be that day was going to be. I actually felt pretty good about it, but knowing what the administrator was looking for can be a whole other thing.

It was now official, I had completed all the requirements for graduation from Southern Connecticut State University and all I had to do now was wait for the Spanish exam test scores to get my diploma. Now that school was over, what was I going to do with regard to Kandice and our relationship? I wasn't planning on leaving her, but I knew that for the next couple months I had to focus on getting in the best shape of my life without any distractions. It was a hard decision, but it was one that had to be made in order to place myself in the best situation mentally and physically to take on this new adventure to the NFL. I decided to go home and wait for the draft and work out with my old high school and college football friends from the area. Kandice wasn't very pleased with that decision, but I told her I would come up periodically and stay with her and her family and work out up there in New Haven, too, and that would have to be the compromise. I had just turned twenty-two years old in March, and I felt like it was time for me to hit the working world. I was no longer a student, and I was getting some last-minute mail from NFL teams. During this waiting period, it got pretty intense as more teams were seeking additional information on me for their database: Denver, New England, Atlanta, the Jets, and a few more teams. New England even said, "We are carefully examining the nation's college talent and we are considering you as a prospect for the National Football League draft on April 28, 1987." It was an endorsement that I was good enough to be drafted and that I had to prepare for what was to become a life-changing experience for my family and myself. March had come and gone; April was here, and at Easter I decided to come up and do Easter with Kandice and her family. I knew for the next couple of weeks and months my time would be unpredictable and uncertain; I had planned to return home on April 26. I made my rounds around the neighborhood and stopped in AL's barbershop where I got my hair cut growing up, and where years earlier, I told Harry Carson, the New York Giants linebacker, he would see me again on the gridiron. I got my usual low-top fade and I was feeling good. Al gave me a good luck wish and I was on my way. I went over to Raymond's house next to see him because he and Rene were the first ones to drop me off at school and football camp; they deserved to get an update of my current status. Raymond wasn't really an athlete like that, but he knew about sports, could play sports, but never played organized due to a hip disability. He spent more time working, arguing with his girl, and telling jokes. He always kept us laughing even in the worst of times, even during the passing of a friend or even parent, he could always find a cheerful memory about the person that he could exaggerate and make us all feel better. He was also a good-looking dude and acted; I had the pleasure of attending Ophelia Devore Modeling School with him my senior year in high school. When I told him of my NFL potential, he broke out in his mix-dancing routine that was a combination of James Brown, George Jefferson, and a drug-high, sixties hipster—all the while moving down his own soul train line. To say the least, he was very happy for me.

I went looking for Icky too. He had just returned from California where he had been living for the past four years. He was different; he had a different attitude and more on-the-edge personality than when he left New Rochelle in 1983. He had partnered with some heavy-duty Columbians involved in some "business dealings" that warranted his robust demeanor and had grown his hair long and Jheri-curled up. He was as big as ever and said that was the look in Cali. He too was happy for me, for it was our dream to play as long as we could, and now I had the opportunity to continue our dream and journey. He would be there in those last weeks before the draft and over the summer preparing me mentally and physically to take the next steps. He made sure I had the do-or-die attitude about the game and not to give a f—— about who was out there, but to knock their heads off—that was his position. I am truly grateful for his friendship and brotherly love over the forty-four years I've know him.

As the day grew nearer, my excitement of the possibility of being drafted grew more. To be drafted would be an honor that only a select few in football history have had the right to claim, and on April 28, 1987, my opportunity was about to come through, I thought. On the 27th of April, I started to watch the countdown on television as they prepared for the draft. Top names were being thrown around, the same names I would watch, myself, on the sports shows and sport television news. I told my mother that the next day would be the draft and that I would know then what our future would be and if I was to be drafted. She was indifferent a bit because she didn't know the process and the magnitude of what it all meant. I tried to reassure her that our lives could change if I got drafted and we could buy a house in a nice area of New Rochelle.

Her response was, "Are you sure you're big enough and are you sure you're good enough?"

I wasn't sure how to take that because mom, on a few occasions, questioned my ability, and now that I had made it this far, my ability was still being questioned. I felt my emotions and temper rising up again, but I held it together for a moment as I sat there in my room crying. Mom new only one thing and that was manual work. She worked the fields in Jamaica as a child and moved to London and worked as a domestic, which continued in America before she started working in food service and as a lunch service worker in the New Rochelle School system. All she knew was to be "good enough" to get and keep a job. It was my hope to make her a believer in me by getting this job as a football player and keeping it.

April 27th was draft day. Although I knew I wouldn't be a high-round draft pick, it was always exciting to watch the draft as a fan, and now possibly getting a call added additional excitement to the day. I believe the draft was being shown on a network station because we didn't have cable television in our house; and I do remember watching most of the early rounds in my room on my black and white television. I believe the first round was televised and the rest was discussed during the sport commentators' analysis and predictions of the players already chosen. It must have been mid-morning when I realized I hadn't received a call yet from any teams. My agent called me from his office to keep me encouraged and positive about the day and to say that anything can happen at any time. As I continued to listen to the sport commentators, they began to speak about the fifth round. The San Diego Chargers were up to make their selection. I remember filling out a questioner for them, so I knew they were interested, or at the very least knew about me. "San Diego Chargers pick Scott Mearsereu from Southern Connecticut State University." That was Scott, my teammate! I was excited and happy for him because him being drafted spoke volumes about Southern's program and that it was a program that produces NFL-qualified players and that there were at least two more Southern players that could possibly hear their names call on April 27!

As time passed, the network broadcast of the draft was about to end, and regular scheduled programing was about to resume. My name hadn't been called on the television broadcast version of the draft, but there were at least seven more rounds to go. At this point, I recognized two defensive backs had been drafted: Rod Woodson from Purdue, who was the number one ranked defensive back coming out this year, and Tim McDonald, a crushing free safety from USC, the number two ranked defensive back this year. I was ranked number twenty-one, which is not a bad number considering the amount of defensive backs that come out every year from all divisions. I was encouraged by my accomplishments as a safety, but was it good enough to get a chance to play on the biggest stage of them all, the National Football League?

Well I wasn't sure after hours had passed and I hadn't received a call. The first day of the draft ended after the sixth round, with the remaining six rounds to commence on April 28. I wont lie, I did feel a little discouraged, knowing that when Mom would return home from work she would ask what happened? And what would she say and feel when I had to tell her I didn't get called. She would say, "Did you play good enough, or you think the coach think you're not good enough?" My dad asked what happened, and I told him tomorrow the draft continues. He said, "Maybe, tomorrow." Man of very few words said something so minor that meant so much. Stay encouraged was the word of the day, and I would stay encouraged no matter what.

The next day on the 28th, the draft continued. This day it was not televised, but viewers were able to stay up to date with the latest draft picks by watching the ticker tape at the bottom of the screen during regular programing. My name hadn't yet been called going into the tenth round, when the Raiders called and wanted to know where I would be in the next half-hour or so. I told them I wasn't going anywhere and that they could reach me at the same number. My heart started to beat fast. Would I be a Raider? Was Mr. Coia impressed with me enough to recommend me as a future Raider? I didn't know for sure, but I was grateful for the call because it still left the possibility open for it to happen. I also received a call from the New York Giants. The Giants had won the Super Bowl that year and there was a lot of excitement in N.Y. around New York. Would I get the chance to suit up with the greatest linebacker, Lawrence Taylor, and Harry Carson, my barbershop comrade? Only time would tell, but first I would have to get picked.

A half-hour went by, then forty-five minutes, then an hour. The draft was over, and I was not picked. I was devastated. What happened? What happened to the Raiders? Because I thought for sure I was going there because they showed the most interest coming to see me so many times and working me out. I wasn't sure what my football career was going to be. I immediately started thinking about finding a job after graduation and returning to school embarrassed. Was my mother right? Was I not good enough? Did the coaches not believe I was good enough? I didn't know what to think; I just knew that my name was not called that day. Kandice called, too, to hear what the status was, and I downplayed the situation and told her that teams are still making decisions, so I didn't know anything yet. Kandice and her family were good supporters of me; her father was the first black quarterback at Southern back in the fifties but was later moved because it was thought that blacks could not play the quarterback position because they lacked the mental capacity for it. I quickly got her off the phone in case she or her father would ask me more questions and I didn't have a good answer—forcing me to make up another lie. But within a few minutes of hanging up with Kandice, the phone rang. It was Chris Mara, the son of the New York Giants owner, Willington Mara, calling me to let me know the New York Giants wanted to sign me. Chris Mara had come to Southern once to meet with me. The Mara family was from New Rochelle, too, and showed some initial interest in me because, I assumed, I was from the neighborhood and I was good enough to play in the NFL. I also didn't think they were all that serious about me because they had just won the Super Bowl and had some veterans on the team who still had a few years under their belts to play.

He asked if I had received any other calls from other teams and I told him the Raiders showed strong interest, but I hadn't heard anything from them that day. I told him that I was interested but I would have to contact my agent and give him the update and have them talk. He said, "Have him call within the next half-hour." A few things went through my head as I hung up the phone. First, what happened around the tenth round that got me knocked out from being picked, as the Raiders insinuated? Two, why did the Giants wait until minutes after the draft to call me and want to sign me? I learned much later that it wasn't what I did, or what I did not do, but it had more to do with what the team needed, and the economics of professional sports. After an hour of conversation between my agent, myself, and the Giant organization, a date was set for me to come in and meet the general manager, Mr. Humes, to sign the negotiated contract, pick up my bonus check, and receive all the information regarding rookie camp, mini-camp, and preseason camp. On May 20, 1987, I drove myself to East Rutherford, New Jersey to complete the signing and become an official member of the New York Football Giants. "I was good enough." Later that day, I met Coach Parcells, Coach Belichick, and the strength coach, Johnny Parker, who was straight from the south with that southern accent and drawl that I first heard on those American cowboy and Indian movies growing up in England.

Chapter Ten

The End Zone

Who would ever think that a little black boy from Paddington, England would have signed a contract to play in the National Football League in 1987; and at the time of my birth, in 1965, it was still illegal to have mixed marriages in parts of America. There many road blocks and walls to climb at my birth, but America has made progress over time and has moved forward in its promise to all its citizens, to creating a land of freedom, justice, liberty, and equality for all. Although America still has much work to be done to fulfill its creed to all its citizens, it is still the one of the few places on earth that provides the freedom and opportunity to pursue an individual's dreams, goals, and aspirations. The biggest influence I would say came from my mother and I am thankful to my mother for taking up the challenge of motherhood. The challenge fulfilled through her faith in a God that he will provide a better life for her and her children and with the hope and dreams of great opportunity and promise. That first light of life that I remembered shining in that dim basement apartment still remains visible in the core of my memory today, reminding me that the future for my children is bright and promising. Staying focused on the light of faith will keep them encouraged and alternately bring them closer to his or her own goals and aspirations. I am an immigrant from the loins of an immigrant living the dream of my wildest imagination, where not many places on earth allow you to do so.

The purpose of this memoir is to have had the reader walk with me on the journey to the NFL. To have the readers, young and old, recognize the potential in all of us to live out his or her own hopes, wishes, dreams, and wants. The journey will not be easy. It will not be without roadblocks and challenges, and even disappointments; but on the other side of these challenges and roadblocks awaits the ultimate prize of fulfillment and achievement. The feeling of accomplishment is a feeling that no sideline commentator can report on, no words can explain, and no picture can describe. It's an inner emotional and personal accomplishment that can only be appreciated by you and those that have travelled that life journey with you. I understand why some athletes return to the neighborhoods from which they came. It is because the people from the neighborhood walked with them along the lonely high way of life before the bright lights of attention crossed their narrow path. The screams of the big stadiums, endorsement deals, and the laughter and companionship of new friends open up new adventures and experiences. I understand that, as an American, I get to choose my friends no matter what their religion, ethnicity, or race. My Italian teammates, my Anglo teammates, Haitian teammates, and my West Indian teammates are all responsible for my rise to the National Football League and I thank them all for their example of excellence in spite of the cultural and social barriers they shouldered every day.

During this journey, I learned much about myself as I continued to grow into my manhood. The early anger issues I had (in spite of the origin), were laid at my feet to get under control, to learn temperance and tolerance. There would be no room for oppositional behavior, discourse, and disruptive behavior if I wanted to meet and reach my dreams. I don't know exactly how I was able to manage my display of anger when off the field but I'm glad I did. It was a good thing, because many great athletes in my time could not make the transition from the field to the community. Few of them ended up dead and some ended in jail. Many great student athletes found themselves being drawn to violent activities that took them far away from the gridiron and their dreams of playing high school football, basketball, and even college. Today, my anger issues are better managed than when I was a child. However, the many years of playing beyond high school has affected my consistency in that regard. Playing at a high level takes a level of anxiety, a level of discourse, and anger to be effective. Mr. Lombardi said, "Football is to be played violently," and to play football any other way—passively—is an oxymoron. I believe living like that for a period of time affects a person emotionally, mentally, as well as physically being. I do believe playing football for such a long time at a high level has affected me in some way. I recognize that now when I coach my son as he pursues his interest in the sport. I find myself coaching him in the way I was taught to play the game and I must quickly catch myself because the game has changed a lot since the '70s and '80s. However, in spite of the game's many changes, a football player must run fast, jump high, and tackle. My position is to hit and tackle the opposition before the whistles blows. My level of expectation comes from my experiences that eventually open doors to college employment or even the National Football League. Having high expectations and aspirations are at the core of the game that makes winners and champions, and the ability to turn "it" off and on when expected to do so.

I've gone back to Paddington only once since my migration to the United States. Experiencing London was such a refreshing feeling as I walked the streets with my family, pointing out the church I went to, the street my soccer ball was punctured, and the flat I nearly burned down. The diversity of the people walking the streets was amazing to see; it reminded me much of the cities New York and Philadelphia. There were people of different hues, different ethnic groups, and races; I would assume religions too. There are so many similarities between England and America, while at the same time, so many differences. Even though I would love to go back for a period of time to London to live, I would rather remain here in America to allow my sons and daughter the multiple opportunities available to them to reach their goals, dreams, and aspirations.

Why the title Before Common Ground?

I titled this memoir not as an autobiography but because I wanted to bring focus and acknowledge those named immigrants I played high school football with. The young men whose families, too, migrated from foreign lands, who brought their children to America hoping for a better life, and from the countries which held soccer as the premier sport of their native land. Many of them like me didn't know anything about American football; and the idea of coming to America and seeking an opportunity to play this unique American sport was far from their aspirations. In contrast to today when we watch the NFL, we see a football field populated with players born in foreign countries as far away as Australia to Africa. The world has changed politically and socially over the past forty years and we have seen an influx of foreign-born players playing in the NFL, consequently letting the world know that America's doors are open to others. Turn on a television today and one will see names from lands far east as Africa to far north as Demark, "Down Under," and even London itself. We shouldn't take for granted the opportunities that others see when they look to America. America is still viewed as the land of opportunity and hope, the land to fulfill hopes and dreams that we all want for children and ourselves. Although we see the diversity of the NFL today from a cultural view point, we must remember there was a time when America and the NFL wasn't as diverse. It was challenging for those early migrants to find themselves welcomed in an Anglo male-dominated society. They fought to be accepted because we spoke funny and fought because we were from other nations and not readily embraced. Today, in much respect much things have improved, and yet much still needs to be done. Today's immigrants come from countries that are at odds with America over political and social issues just like when I migrated to America forty-four years ago. The issues remain the same: dictators and countries with social and economic breakdowns as the world looks on. And still the world looks to America as the place of refuge and hope. Out of the constant world transformations and amongst the influx of refugees and migrants, who will be the next "Patrick Morrison" to live out their American Dream in a world of opportunity and possibilities that will open up to them? When that immigrant turns on his or her television set and watches men and women of different backgrounds jumping high, running fast, building structures, and flying planes, what unshakable impression will it leave in their minds that will provide hope and promise of a better life and better future for their family?

I am thankful for the many people who have been in the "village" of New Rochelle. I am thankful for the memories of those who have supported me through my difficult times, and those who have been there to cheer me on during those memorable moments as well. To cousin Clive, who demonstrated that you didn't have to be 6 6" and born in the America to dominate in an

American sport. To Coach Bailey and Mr. Holley (may they rest in peace), who taught me the inner instinct needed to play the game of football. To Joe Fosina, who drove me to my college recruiting trips and supported me with conversation and direction on what to do next in my life journey; who opened his house to me and all the youth tackle players forty years ago and remains open today. Thank you! To Rene and Raymond, who provided laughter all the way to New Haven, Connecticut, keeping me calm as they dropped me off at college my first day because I wasn't sure how to get there. I am thankful to Southern Connecticut State University and my Southern teammates for making my four years an unforgettable experience. "Through these doors walk the most dedicated football players in New England." To Sonny Fernandez, who convinced me to attend Southern, mentored me throughout my career, taught me how to play defensive back, and how to be the best college football player I could ever be. To the two finest college coaches who have had the most significant impact in my life, Kevin Gilbride and Rich Cavanaugh; you both met me as a rough-around-the-edges, undisciplined boy, and are responsible for transforming me into the more focused and determined man. I am grateful for you pushing me, correcting me, and running me—instilling a harder work ethic, sacrifice of self, and commitment; because of that you made me a better player and a better person today. Last but not least, my mother, Imogene Lucilda Morrison-Bailey, who decided to take a chance on a dream in 1971 and come to America to start a new life for herself and her children. I thank God for allowing me to have taken this journey with her and be one of the first to play on "uncommon ground" in the National Football League. Mom, you believed in your dream and set, and demonstrated the commitment needed to be self-reliant and self-sufficient, having faith in your God in a country that allowed you to. At times I may have been stubborn, forgetful and angry; you were patient and trusted in a higher power to intercede, and he did. God blessed me with you and I thank him for you.

God bless you all and God bless, protect, and guide those immigrants who dream of working and playing on "Uncommon Ground."

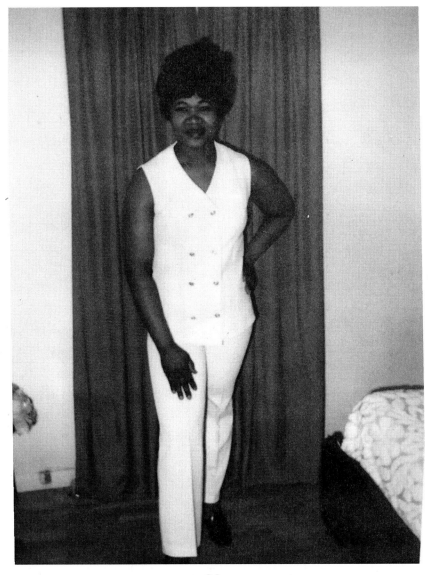

Mom

Brother Michael

August 1974

Cub Scouts

Second Childhood Home

YTL MVP Trophy

Southern '85

1982

1976

High School, 1983

Defensive MVP 1983 McKenna Award

Me 1987

Jr. Banquet

College 1986

McKenna Award 1983

My High School

First Home in America, 2nd floor room, 140 Washington Ave.

Stepdad John Bailey

Lue and Pat Aptil '72

Pat and Sister

Cleve and Me and Terrance

Giants Parking Jersey 1986 - Rookie Camp

New Rochelle SPort Hall of Fame

1980 Championship Game - T-Fudge, Me, Icky, Hubert

Me

New Rochelle